Praise for *Confessions of a Good Christian Guy*

"Tom Davis knows that no Christian guy can be truly good unless he's honest enough to confess—or come clean—that he's not always so good. A refreshing and honest guide for men seeking true friends and personal integrity."

—Brian McLaren
Author and Activist, www.brianmclaren.net

"Kudos to Tom Davis and Tammy Maltby for honestly addressing the struggles that Christian men face in the 21st century. *Confessions of a Good Christian Guy* serves as a powerful reminder that our gracious Heavenly Father routinely works in spite of our brokenness, imperfection, and sin to transform us into the likeness of Christ. This is essential reading for any man ready to take an honest look at himself and willing to allow God to change him from the inside out."

—Jim Daly
President, Focus on the Family

"Brace yourself! *Confessions of a Good Christian Guy* is not just another 'I-used-to-have-problems-but-now-I'm-fixed' feel-good fantasy. No, this is solid intelligence. Davis and Maltby take us on a tour of the front lines that run through every church, every family, and the life of every man. His assessment is honest and wise. You will find hope in these pages, and the comfort that comes from knowing that you are not alone."

—Nate Larken
Author of *Samson and the Pirate Monks*

"Tom Davis sets the tone when he declares at the end of Chapter One, 'I choose not to lie anymore.' *Raw*—from telling the truth of his own life. *Real*—from the foundation of telling the truth from Biblical stories of men struggling. *Redemptive*—from telling the truth about grace that we, as men, long to not just simply know about but daily live. And a critical fourth "R": *Relationship*. You cannot become the man you need and want to be all by yourself. This book will remind you, again and again, where change needs to take place in your life, and offers you the first steps to getting there."

—Wes Roberts
Founder/CCO, Leadership Design Group

"FINALLY! A book that hits the essential issues facing men today and also gives practical insights on how to experience true life-change. Tom Davis has done a courageous and masterful job—this is a must read for all men."

—Vince D'Acchioli
Founder, On Target Ministries

"Transparency is so needed in the heart of the church, and Tom rings out a clear call for us to stop pretending that everything's okay, because it's not! As a worship leader and songwriter, I'm amazed at the pull towards being 'fake' when we show up to church— when church is the one place where we should be totally free to confess our humanity and support each other. That's why I wrote the words 'just as you are' in 'Come now is the time to worship'. Tom—through his own shortcomings and clear biblical teaching—encourages us to stop pretending and be set free!"

—Brian Doerksen
Songwriter

CONFESSIONS

OF A
GOOD CHRISTIAN GUY

TOM DAVIS
AND TAMMY MALTBY

THOMAS NELSON
Since 1798

NASHVILLE DALLAS MEXICO CITY RIO DE JANEIRO BEIJING

Published in Nashville, Tennessee, by Thomas Nelson. Thomas Nelson is a trademark of Thomas Nelson, Inc.

Published in association with William K. Jensen Literary Agency, 119 Bampton Court, Eugene, OR 97474.

To protect the privacy of individuals, some names and details have been changed, and some stories are composite characters.

Thomas Nelson, Inc. titles may be purchased in bulk for educational, business, fund-raising, or sales promotional use. For information, please e-mail SpecialMarkets@ThomasNelson.com.

All Scripture quotations, unless otherwise indicated, are taken from The Holy Bible, New International Version. © 1973, 1978, 1984, International Bible Society. Used by permission of Zondervan Bible Publishing House.

Scripture quotations noted CEV are taken from the Contemporary English Version, © 1995 by the American Bible Society. Used by permission.

Scripture quotations noted MSG are taken from *The Message* by Eugene H. Peterson. © 1993, 1994, 1995, 1996, 2000, 2001, 2002. Used by permission of NavPress Publishing Group. All rights reserved.

Scripture quotations noted NASB are taken from New American Standard Bible, © 1960, 1977, 1995 by the Lockman Foundation. Used by permission.

Scripture quotations noted NLT are taken from The Holy Bible, New Living Translation®, © 1996. Used by permission of Tyndale House Publishers, Inc., Wheaton, IL 60189. All rights reserved.

Library of Congress Cataloging-in-Publication Data

Davis, Tom, 1934-
    Confessions of a good Christian guy / Tom Davis and Tammy Maltby.
      p. cm.
    Includes bibliographical references.
    ISBN 978-0-7852-2806-6 (pbk.)
    1. Christian men--Religious life. 2. Davis, Tom, 1934- I. Maltby, Tammy. II. Title.
BV4528.2.D387 2007
248.8'42--dc22

2007027598

Printed in the United States of America

08 09 10 11 RRD 9 8 7 6 5 4 3 2

To my grandfather, Herbert Bradley Branham,
for modeling to me what a real man looks like.
—Tom Davis

•••

To my father, Ken W. Hanson.
Thank you for giving me life and for
your loving devotion toward your family.
Thank you for being faithful and honorable to
Mom for nearly fifty-eight years.
You did so much right, Dad. I am very blessed.

To my son, Samuel CJ Maltby.
May you continue to become a man of valor and strength,
defending those who have no power, protecting those
who are lost. This mother could not love a son more than you.
—Tammy Maltby

HE WHO CONCEALS HIS SINS
DOES NOT PROSPER,
WHOEVER CONFESSES AND RENOUNCES
THEM FINDS MERCY.
—PROV. 28:13

CONTENTS

ACKNOWLEDGMENTS

First, thanks to my incredible wife, Emily, and all our children: Anya, Hayden, Gideon, Gracie, Lilly, and Hudson. You are the ones who pay the price when I'm writing a book. I love you all and am so thankful for your support.

A special thank-you to Tammy Maltby. You believed in this project, you believed in me, and this book has become a reality. Marcus Brotherton, it has truly been a joy and honor to work with you. Thanks for all your insight and coaching. Bill Jensen, thanks for trusting me with the men's book. Joey Paul, thanks for your encouragement and insight.

To the staff at Children's HopeChest, who share my life and passions: George, Matt, Rachel, Sam, Deanne, Dany, Ira, Julie, Debbie, Elizabeth, and Lena (who is more like a daughter than a coworker).

To Nate Larkin, for going the extra mile to help me and to find men willing to share their stories. I couldn't have done it without you, my friend—thanks.

Thanks to Vince D'Acchioli, for encouraging me on the

journey. To Ed Bissonette, for being a friend and companion. To Dr. Bob Grant, for being an example to me of what a real man looks like. To Wes Roberts, for your love and care for my family and me. To Brett Irwin, for being a true friend and brother. To Dwayne Black, for the gift of adoption!

To Craig Whittaker—a man I greatly admire and look up to—thanks for being a huge part of my life. John Cressman, your friendship is a great gift to me. Jim Fitzgerald, thanks for your camaraderie and for being a living example of what it means to give.

Thanks to all the men who had the courage and vulnerability to share the pain and victories of their lives. May the fruit of your reward be the transformation of the lives of many men.

To the continued dream of what covenant and manhood means. Gary Black, Seth Barnes, and Andrew Shearman, I love you men and am more excited each day as the adventure of life unfolds before us.

—Tom Davis
Colorado Springs, Colorado

PASSING THE BATON

TAMMY MALTBY

It was a beautiful, warm Mother's Day in Colorado when a knock came on my door. Tom Davis stood there. I had never met him before. He knew some friends of ours and wanted to buy a home in our neighborhood. Little did I realize the provision and sovereignty of God at that moment. I now know God's tender fingerprints were all over that introduction.

Tom and his wife, Emily, became fast friends with us. Funny how first impressions are so limiting. I thought Tom was just a typical good Christian guy. President of a ministry that helps orphans in Russia (a big deal to me because I have a daughter adopted from Russia), Tom is smart, well traveled, and seems to have it all together. Emily is absolutely gorgeous and manages their busy and loving home well. They are a great young Christian couple with a bunch of kids—so I assumed they were your basic Christian magazine cover: zipped up . . . cleaned up . . . looking good for Jesus.

It wasn't until several months later, while having dinner in my home, that I heard Tom's full story: he had experienced much sorrow due to his own sin and the sin that had been done against him. As I listened to his story, I was mesmerized. Not only was he the best storyteller around (no kidding!), but I was profoundly moved by Tom's honesty, transparency, and genuine brokenness. In a world that seems to celebrate anything but that, I thought, *How does he get away with this? Doesn't he know you're not supposed to let others know about your weaknesses—particularly in the Christian community?* I was intrigued.

In fact, the love I had for Tom and Emily grew even more because of what they had walked through and the way they had chosen to be real about their pain and redemption. They had seasoned and matured through unbelievably difficult situations and still chose to walk with the Lord and to love His church. Instead of isolating themselves, Tom and Emily shared their story and lives within their community. I was deeply impressed. They seemed about as real as real could be: honest, loving, fun, and authentic.

Our families became much closer as time went on. Tom became like a brother to me; Emily a sister. I was present at the birth of their daughter (which was one of the most amazing experiences of my life, I might add!). A few years ago when I went through one of the darkest seasons of my life, Tom and Emily were there for me like no other: consistent, steady, longsuffering. I consider them my closest friends and, in a true sense, my real family today.

A Voice to Trust

Last year as I wrote *Confessions of a Good Christian Girl,*[1] I sensed the Lord leading me to work on another book, this one geared toward men's issues. I knew some of the ideas in the book could be mine, but I wasn't the person to write it. Men would want to hear directly from a man. It couldn't be just anyone either; he would have to be a specific kind of author. He would need to understand both pain and the miraculous grace of God. The author would need an amazing ability to embrace people wherever they are, no matter what they're going through.

As I thought and prayed, I knew Tom Davis was the man to spearhead the message of this book. Tom's been there. He knows what it's like to encounter the unrelenting, outrageous grace of God. I'm passing the challenge of this book, like a baton, on to Tom. The places he'll journey with you in the pages ahead are raw, real, and redemptive. He's the best runner I know.

As Tom and I discussed the tone and tenor of this book, we acknowledged this would be a book predominately read by men, but women would read it too. We want to encourage this. One of the central themes of these pages is that no one is truly isolated. We need others around us to spur us along, to elevate and affirm us. We're a family, brothers and sisters in the Lord. That sense of community is essential to our walk as believers.

With this in mind, I've written a brief reflection at the end of each chapter to help all of us—men and women—think not just as individuals, but as people connected with one another. For men reading this book, maybe you aren't specifically struggling with a topic in a certain chapter, but you have a friend who is. These reflections will help you know what you can do. For women reading this book, these short sections invite us to think about how we can support our brothers, husbands, sons, fathers, grandfathers, and male friends. That's the spirit in which these are written: not to direct, preach at, fix, or correct anybody—but to ask how we can walk alongside those we care about.

Each of these short sections includes a reflection on the chapter's main ideas, a Bible verse, and a brief closing thought. I encourage you to think of these sections as opportunities for reflection and action.

Overall, this book is an invitation to let Jesus Christ lead us all in a good direction. It's true, this book is a confession, and confession involves sin. But the real message of this book is God's grace. How do we even begin to describe God's grace? God's grace is simply amazing, outrageous, enormous—it's almost too good to be true. I guess that's why they call it the *good news,* for even the most desperate situations are opportunities for God's marvelous, magnificent, and yes, outstanding grace.

In his book *The Ragamuffin Gospel,* Brennan Manning describes it this way: "The gospel of grace announces: Forgiveness precedes repentance. The sinner is accepted before he pleads for mercy. It is already granted. He need only receive it. Total amnesty. Gratuitous pardon."[2]

This journey before us is to discover this amazing grace of Jesus Christ. This grace is already granted to us. We need only receive it. I invite you along.

—Tammy Maltby
Monument, Colorado

CHAPTER 1

CONFESSIONS
A Courageous Look at the Secrets Inside Us

My name is Tom Davis, and I'm a good Christian guy.

Let me tell you a bit about my life.

I've been married to Emily—the most wonderful woman in the world—for eleven years. We have six beautiful children, including an adopted daughter from Russia. I'm a good father. I work as the president of an international organization that helps orphans. In addition, I'm a leadership development consultant for midlevel to Fortune 500 companies. I'm a good provider for my family. I go to church. I read my Bible. By the grace of God, I wake up every morning excited about living.

I've also slept with countless women, snorted cocaine, stolen cash from people, and spent time in jail.

Here's the real surprise—all that stuff happened *after* I became a Christian.

Like I say, my name is Tom Davis, and I'm a good Christian guy.

This is my confession.

LIVING WITH SECRETS

Perhaps you have a similar story—maybe not with sins as glaring as mine, but there are issues in your life you wish were hidden. Maybe it's something in your past. Maybe it's happening today. Has anything like this ever happened to you?

- Driving home from church, some idiot cuts you off on the freeway. So you speed up, give him the bird, and cut *him* off. The jerk! One minute you're humming praise songs, the next minute you want to hurt someone. What gives?
- Last night you were checking your e-mail, and an ad for a singles' Web site popped up. You clicked on it (just to check what's out there these days) and saw another link. You spent the next two hours looking at porn. You feel horrible.
- You live a pretty clean life, but one time back in college things really got out of hand. It was spring break, you had too much to drink, and things took a nasty turn. Man, if anybody found out about that today, it wouldn't be good.

Ouch. This isn't us. Our desire as good Christian guys is to love the Lord, to work hard; to support our families, churches, and communities; and to be examples to others. We pride ourselves on walking the line.

But if we look at our lives honestly, we recognize some

facades. Underneath are a host of harmful realities—hidden thoughts, nagging memories, bad decisions, broken dreams, shattered goals. Sometimes we feel mired in a pit.

It's not that we aren't outwardly successful. Many of us have good jobs and great families. We're respected in our neighborhoods and communities. At church, we're ushers and deacons and youth sponsors and worship leaders and Sunday school teachers—we're the ones shaking hands at the door with smiles on our faces. We're not backsliders or apostates or pagans or nonbelievers. We're good Christian guys, and churches are filled with men like us.

It's our inner lives that hold problems. Either there's sin in our past we want to keep quiet, or else we keep on sinning, often secretly. This nagging darkness in our inner lives stymies us.

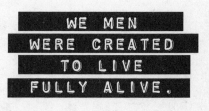

WE MEN WERE CREATED TO LIVE FULLY ALIVE.

Many of us grew up hearing stories of black-and-white conversions—*once I was lost; now I'm found.* We're used to thinking of Christianity in terms of before-and-after stories. The implication is that once a person has found Christ, his life should be tidy afterward. Now that we're believers, our slate is supposed to be wiped completely clean. But for some reason, our yuck is still there. In our honest moments, we admit there are huge places of deadwood in our lives—places of decay we wish weren't there.

We know a better way exists. In John 10:10, Jesus Christ says, "I have come that they may have life, and have it to the full." We men were created to live fully alive. Christ wants us to be fully alive in our relationships, fully alive in our jobs, fully alive in our places of service. This is who we're meant to be. But somehow we're not truly living this abundant life, so we try harder to clean ourselves up.

We pray for relief . . . but it doesn't come.

We read self-help books . . . but the quick-fix answers are just annoying.

We beg God to be rescued . . . but our behavior doesn't change at all.

That's what happened in my own life. I was a Christian, trying to live by my own standards, and my life was a mess. I had

THIS IS A FACT: GOOD CHRISTIAN GUYS DO END UP IN THE WRONG PLACES DOING THE WRONG THINGS.

walked the aisle of a Southern Baptist church at the ripe age of ten in Midland, Texas, complete with choir singing "Just As I Am" in the background. I could argue the doctrine of "once saved, always saved" with the best of them. I knew if I died—and I was really pushing the limits at times—I would go straight to heaven because Jesus paid the price for my sins. I *believed*. But by no means was I living an abundant life.

Why was I living so low? What was so awful about my life that it drove me to regularly practice destructive behavior? Why wasn't my life working as it was supposed to?

That was the question I was desperately trying to figure out.

That's the question I know many of you are wrestling with.

BEYOND CLUB DEADWOOD

This is a fact: good Christian guys *do* end up in the wrong places doing the wrong things. The Bible is filled with stories of men who had hearts for God and still blew it.

Abraham was a liar.

Jonah ran away from his responsibility.

David—one of the greatest kings of Israel—had an affair with a married woman and then ordered the murder of her husband. You can't get much worse than that.

We're in good company with our deadwood. I don't say that to minimize sin. I say that as reality. When you sit in church and take a good look around you, everyone (and I do mean *everyone*) has done things—*and is doing things*—he or she isn't proud of.

The first response is often to shrug off our responsibility. It's easy to pass the buck when it comes to sin. Men are fabulous at this. Maybe our boss is heavy-handed, so it drives us to drink. Or our dad was a jerk, so he's responsible for our failures today.

I have a good friend who is an alcoholic. This guy loves the Lord, but his life is completely out of control. He's caught in a vicious cycle of traveling, drinking, lying, being alone, drinking, drinking, and more drinking. His world is falling apart, but he won't yet accept responsibility for his actions. It's too easy to point the finger at everyone else.

For many years I pointed a finger at others for my problems. I acted the way I did because of my pain. And I could come up with a stockpile of reasons my pain was there: feelings of aban-donment, rejection, confusion, lack of direction. Maybe I did what I did as a cover-up for how horrible I felt about myself because of what I suffered as a child, or because of my rebellious actions as an adult, or both. My pain was real, and I was in numbing, acting-out mode because of my pain—but that still doesn't give me an excuse for sin.

I know this for sure: we kill every chance of living a fully alive life if we refuse to accept responsibility for our actions. Everyone has pain. Pain is universal. When we're in numbing, acting-out mode, we'll attempt anything to deaden the pain in our souls—fill in the blank as to what your issue might be. But if we good Christian guys don't learn to accept responsibility for our actions *despite* our pain, we'll never move forward. We hurt, we struggle, we're disappointed with ourselves, we feel like failures, and we act out. But still, it's us doing the acting out. No matter how the pain got there, we have to accept responsibility for what we do.

> **WE KILL EVERY CHANCE OF LIVING A FULLY ALIVE LIFE IF WE REFUSE TO ACCEPT RESPONSIBILITY FOR OUR ACTIONS.**

Sometimes, even, we have to come to the end of a rope before anything changes. I call that the place of despair—a place without hope. I came to that place. At one point, I actually hated my life. The strange news is that despair can actually be a gift, because it can be a motivator. It can slice through our pretenses, show us our need, and make us willing to do whatever it takes to change directions. If we let it, despair can drive us into the arms of God.

What's your level of despair? On a scale of one to ten, how desperate are you right now? Are you at rock bottom? Or do you feel a few steps away? Maybe life isn't all it's meant to be, but you could continue in your pattern a long time before you reach the bottom.

Guess what? All are places of despair. There is no hope when you're heading down a path toward death. Left unchecked, where will your actions lead you in five years? Ten years? Tomorrow? What relationships will be harmed? What job will you lose? What ministry position will you be unable to fulfill?

God's invitation to us is to choose life. When we realize our despair, we become willing to give up our quest to be the best Christian guy ever and let God remake us into the kind of sons He wants.

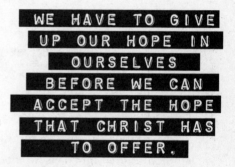

WE HAVE TO GIVE UP OUR HOPE IN OURSELVES BEFORE WE CAN ACCEPT THE HOPE THAT CHRIST HAS TO OFFER.

When we acknowledge our despair, or when we give up pretending to be somebody we're not, we start to put our trust in God, where it belongs. We have to give up our hope in ourselves before we can accept the hope that Christ has to offer.

Ezekiel 47 gives us a picture of what God is able to do with the deadwood in our lives. Ezekiel describes a new city of God with a river flowing out from a new temple. The city is surrounded by dead things, but everywhere the water runs becomes alive again. The water heals and restores everything. The water is a picture of the Holy Spirit. The Holy Spirit gives us a new kind of living. The real miracle is God's constant pursuit of us, even while we are sinners. God brings things back to life again.

My prayer for us as men is that we will accept responsibility for the deadwood in our lives and open up a crack for the Spirit of God to get in. The crack is an admission of our brokenness; it's the end of the superficial image we've tried to present; it's admitting our failures—as hard as that is for men. That crack can widen and expand, allowing God's healing water to restore us to the abundant life we were meant to lead. We don't deserve it. But Christ promises abundant life by His grace.

THE GOOD NEWS OF GRACE

That's the real message of this book—we good Christian guys need that grace.

We needed it when we first came to Christ, and we continue to need it even now that we're believers. At the end of the day, the grace of Jesus Christ is the only thing we have to count on. Sure, we have responsibility to own up to our sin. We need to take steps toward accountability, toward safeguarding our lives, and toward running with perseverance the race marked for us.

But at the end of the day, it's always God's grace that saves us. It's always God's grace that leads us to the lives we were meant to lead. We good Christian guys need grace as much as any unbeliever does.

Grace doesn't mean that we need to "snuggle up in the lap of Jesus"—that type of warm, fuzzy thinking doesn't work for most men. And grace never gives us a license to lie down on the job or get sloppy with our lives. "Shall we go on sinning so that grace may increase?" the apostle Paul asks. "By no means! We died to sin; how can we live in it any longer?" (Rom. 6:1). Christ calls us to own up to our sin.

Rather, the message of grace is that God is rock solid in His commitment to us. He never gives up on us. Never. Christ saves us when we turn to Him, and He never leaves us, even when we're sinning. Christ is the One who truly heals and restores us and leads us to a place of abundant living. It takes our responsibility—yes, but ultimately, He's the One who lifts us out of the deadwood and into fully alive lives.

When I think of the message of grace, I think of Romans 7 and 8. We have to take these two chapters of the Bible together.

In Romans 7, Paul talks about all the mistakes he makes and the struggles he has with sinning. He tries all the time to do what he should, but he always seems to do the opposite of that. He keeps sinning. And sinning some more.

Then in Romans 8:1, Paul makes this amazingly strong statement: "There is now no condemnation for those who are in Christ Jesus." No condemnation. None whatsoever. That's grace. And that's our invitation—to continually remind ourselves of that truth. In spite of our sins, we aren't condemned.

Grace. It sounds so simple, but it can be one of the hardest ideas to fully grasp.

Grace begins by believing that somehow God can turn our messy secrets into something better. It begins with understanding the reality that Christ died for sinners—which includes all of us good Christian guys, as well as those who don't know Him at all. It begins when we open our eyes, our minds, and our hearts in wonder to His grace.

In the end, it's all about grace.

Loving, forgiving, fully alive grace.

Strengthening, overwhelming, truly amazing grace.

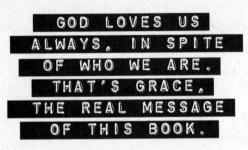

GOD LOVES US ALWAYS, IN SPITE OF WHO WE ARE. THAT'S GRACE, THE REAL MESSAGE OF THIS BOOK.

That type of grace is the reason I've written this book in the first place. Because in so many ways, grace is the story of my life— and I want to tell you why. So this book is my confession to you about times I've lost my way. And about the many times I have been sought out and rescued by a persistent, always strong God.

God loves us always, in spite of who we are.

That's grace, the real message of this book.

A FULLY ALIVE INVITATION

What kind of a God doesn't condemn us in spite of our sins? What kind of God runs, not *from* us, but *to* us, even when we might be a long way off?

That's the type of God we're invited to experience.

One night as a young man, I had mixed a cocktail of all the drugs in my apartment and was busy trying to snort myself happy. In the midst of tears and hopelessness and a bleeding nose, God spoke to me. I knew it was God—though His voice wasn't audible, His message was clear: *Do you remember the story of the Prodigal Son? Go back and read it.*

I started tearing through boxes, looking under furniture, hurling books off the bookshelf in search of a Bible. I finally found it, the one my grandparents gave me as a child. I turned to the Gospel of Luke:

Once a man had two sons. The younger son said to his father, "Give me my share of the property." So the father divided his property between his two sons.

Not long after that, the younger son packed up everything he owned and left for a foreign country, where he wasted all his money in wild living. He had spent everything, when a bad famine spread through that whole land. Soon he had nothing to eat.

He went to work for a man in that country, and the man sent him out to take care of his pigs. He would have been glad to eat what the pigs were eating, but no one gave him a thing. Finally, he came to his senses and said, "My father's workers have plenty to eat, and here I am, starving to death! I will go to my father and say to him, 'Father, I have sinned against God in heaven and against you. I am no longer good enough to be called your son. Treat me like one of your workers.'"

The younger son got up and started back to his father. But when he was still a long way off, his father saw him and felt sorry for him. He ran to his son and hugged and kissed him. The son said, "Father, I have sinned against God in heaven and against you. I am no longer good enough to be called your son."

But his father said to the servants, "Hurry and bring the best clothes and put them on him. Give him a ring for his finger and sandals for his feet. Get the best calf and prepare it, so we can eat and celebrate. This son of mine was dead, but has now come back to life. He was lost and has now been found." And they began to celebrate. (vv. 11–24 CEV)

As I read that familiar passage, tears streamed down my face. I felt like that passage was written for me. It described exactly how I felt.

I had run off and wasted everything in wild living.

I was living in the midst of the pigpen.

I sinned and didn't feel worthy.

But the Father ran to the young man . . . hugged him and kissed him, put the best clothes on him, and gave him the signet ring. The young man was home and forgiven, restored and renewed.

That's what God was doing to me in that very moment. He spoke to me through the story. I was beginning to feel like a new man! I was experiencing the Father heart of God—right there in the midst of my ruin.

That's the type of God we're invited to experience!

In the pages ahead, we'll take a look at a God who can change our lives into something we never dreamed possible. We'll take a look at how God encountered some good Christian guys who were literally at the end of themselves physically, emotionally, and spiritually. These stories tell us a lot about what God can do with people who have deadwood in their lives. These stories offer clear views of abundant lives in action.

This book is not meant to be a shocking exposé but an honest and courageous look at some of the secrets that often lurk behind a victorious Christian facade—secrets that range from sexual sins to anger to addictions to thoughts of suicide.

Throughout the book, we'll see a strong testimony of the Lord's eagerness to cleanse and heal those who turn to Him.

There's also a strong invitation to us to own up to the sin, brokenness, and shame in our midst—within the church as well as outside—and to extend to each other the same persistent and healing grace that Jesus extends to us. Think of this book as your key to genuine, safe accountability. That's the beginning of change.

> THINK OF THIS BOOK AS YOUR KEY TO GENUINE, SAFE ACCOUNTABILITY. THAT'S THE BEGINNING OF CHANGE.

The invitation contained in these pages is your call to a fully alive life. Think of it: God really does have an amazing plan for *your* life. God's method of working in the world has always been to use people: Adam, Abraham, Moses, David, John the Baptist, Matthew, Peter, Paul.

A lot of these guys in the Bible are just like us, bound up in the worst junk possible, but God extends His plan to them—and to us—in ways unimaginable. Those men went through some of the exact same things many of us go through. They led secret lives of sin. But they came to a point where they gave up their performances.

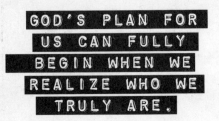

GOD'S PLAN FOR US CAN FULLY BEGIN WHEN WE REALIZE WHO WE TRULY ARE.

They all came to the place where they allowed the Spirit of God into their lives. And when they did, they became the great men we know of today.

God's plan for us can fully begin when we realize who we truly are. We are called to eternal, incredible, kingdom-oriented living. When we choose life and not death, we can live the abundant life God calls us to. Henry David Thoreau famously observed that most men live lives of quiet desperation. But that doesn't have to be us. God's grace is sufficient and available right now. God can give us the power to live a new, incredible life.

Maybe you think that could never be you. *That may be fine for others,* you think, *but I'll stay with what I'm used to—even if that continues to hurt me.*

I was like that once. I lived a life so far from abundant it brought me to the very brink of crime, jail, even suicide.

But if God can transform someone like me, He can bring new life to anyone. My story isn't pretty, but it's real.

THE LURE OF A PINK HOTEL

The Hotel Pink.

Don't laugh; that's what it was called.

One light hung down like in a prison cell. Two rusted beds squatted in the corners. An icy draft came through the walls. The pink paint on the walls was peeling off to reveal several colors underneath, including a dark, yellow muck.

Did someone pee on the wall? I thought. *Better not touch anything in here.*

The Hotel Pink existed for two purposes: drugs and hookers. I couldn't believe I was here. Shame swept through my soul. I hoped nobody would ever find out about this.

I had come to the Hotel Pink with another guy for both reasons. My friend had just done time in the Big House for burglary and drug possession. Good company. We were in search of cocaine—"snow" or "nose candy," as it was called on the streets. Neither of us were strangers to the drug, but we weren't interested in putting it up our noses this time. We needed a new rush tonight, so for the first time, we planned to mainline it. Mainlining cocaine is when the drug is boiled down to its most potent form and then spiked into your veins through a hypodermic needle. It produces a more intense, crazy high. The nutty part about this is that I thought it was a good idea.

My friend gathered the stuff. I sat on one of the rusty beds and wrapped a belt around my arm. The cocaine slowly disappeared into my vein. The effect hit immediately. The room began to spin, and my heart beat a million miles an hour. I thought I was going to die. I begged my friend not to do it. My eyes rolled back in my head, my words slurred, and saliva poured out of the corner of my mouth. (Drugs are so glamorous.) "Don't try it, please," I urged my friend. "It's too much! I'm going over the edge . . ."

Enter the prostitute, stage left. She had been scheduled to come just after we got high. She wore a miniskirt and a low-cut blouse. On her arm were dozens of bracelets, and she wore gaudy, dangling earrings. She slunk over to one of the rusty beds, pouted to us with her red-lipsticked face, and beckoned.

I was a Christian.

How had I ever sunk to such a low?

Trace my life back.

I never knew my real father. My mom remarried when I was a kid. My stepfather was an abusive, hitting, insulting alcoholic. One of my first memories is at age six. My mom and I came home to find my stepfather passed out on the front porch. We considered waking him to move him into the house, but we knew if we did he'd hit us both. Several times, my mom packed up everything and left him. Yet for some reason she always came back. The one bright spot is that every time my mom left my stepfather, she'd let me stay with my grandparents. And my grandparents knew Jesus Christ.

Without a doubt, I accepted Christ into my heart through my grandparents' influence. I walked to church anytime I could. But I could never quite understand God. I remember at thirteen crying myself to sleep because my stepfather had just beat me up again. God was all-powerful. He could have stopped my step-father's abuse. But He didn't. *That must mean God doesn't like me for some reason,* I remember thinking.

In high school I had a friend whose dad was theologically astute—or at least he talked like he was. He took a really hard-line approach on eternal security. It didn't really matter what we did, he said, because we were saved no matter what. I know now that eternal security is a good, biblically based doctrine, but for a kid like me looking to push the envelope, what my friend's dad said to me sounded like a license to do anything I wanted. Incidentally, this same man later had an affair with his fifteen-year-old housecleaner. So much for astute theology.

Toward the end of high school and in early college, I pressed into alcohol and drugs for relief. I had always drunk alcohol, just a bit. I remember stealing booze as young as eleven. But this was a whole new level of indulgence. When I was high, I didn't feel my pain as much. Alcohol turned to pot, then speed, acid, ecstasy, coke, and finally meth. Several times I tried to get off drugs and be "a good person." I even led a Bible study with my drug friends for a while. We'd put a big pile of cocaine on the coffee table and open Scripture together while getting high. I wish I could tell you this was an effective form of evangelism, but I can't recall it ever working.

You can only maintain insanity on this level for so long. Your mind starts to blur. You get paranoid beyond anything you've ever experienced. Life's a mess. I knew what the right thing to do was. I knew Jesus wasn't honored by my behavior. I knew the truth. But try as hard as I might, I couldn't change. Have you ever been there? You want to change so badly, but you keep returning to what is destroying you. Second Peter 2:22 described me perfectly: "A dog will come back to lick up its own vomit. A pig that has been washed will roll in the mud" (CEV).

Several times I went to church and tried to straighten out my life, but I'd always find myself dropping acid the next weekend. I swore I would never get drunk again on a Sunday morning and would find myself blitzed out of my mind two weeks later. I could only do the right thing for so long. I could only temporarily keep it together and "be holy," as the preachers kept saying. I was so miserable I wanted to give up living. Have you ever been there?

The duplicitous lifestyle was slowly killing me. I drank more, partied more, did more drugs, and died inside a little more each day. But I would sink to one more low before I would allow any change to truly happen.

My new low was greed.

Besides cocaine and a storehouse of other boutique drugs, the thrill of beating the system also rushed through my veins. I loved the thought of getting something for nothing. I also loved the buzz I got off of making The Man pay.

I had always been quick in school, graduating from high school at age sixteen. Early on, I worked for a telemarketer. I figured I could do it on my own and make a lot more money. So I got a business partner, and we started an enterprise designed with one goal in mind: to put a lot of cash in our pockets as quickly as possible.

Have you ever received a card in the mail that said something like this?

YOU ARE ABSOLUTELY GUARANTEED ONE OF THE FOLLOWING AWARDS FOR PARTICIPATING IN OUR NATIONAL PROMOTION!

A Brand-New Lincoln Navigator

A $10,000 Cashier's Check

A 10-Carat Genuine Diamond and Sapphire Tennis Bracelet

A $2,000 United States Savings Bond

1-800-555-5555. Call today!

Please don't hate me. This business began legally, but it was designed to thrive off people's ignorance.

Our business proved to be a cash cow. Thousands of people called to sign up. Each caller was required to invest a small upfront fee—four hundred to six hundred dollars—for which most received the beautiful ten-carat tennis bracelet. Yes, it was real; yes, it did come with a certificate of authenticity; and yes, we imported it from Taiwan for thirty-three bucks. The scam was a bit more complex than that, but you get the picture.

Everything worked beautifully for a while. Money rolled in. At age twenty, I owned a big house in Houston, an apartment on the other side of town for extra deals, a brand-new sports car, and a closet full of thousand-dollar suits. Money was everything.

But one day the good people at Visa and MasterCard caught wind of what we were doing and shut down our merchant accounts. Without these accounts, we couldn't fulfill our orders. Our business was ruined. But we had grown accustomed to our extravagant lifestyle.

It was time to get desperate.

What choice did we have but to beat the system? If you're good enough with a computer, you can copy anything. What you can't copy, you can scan with laser perfection. So that's what my business partner and I did. The telemarketing business we were in had records of every customer we had ever done business with. They had given us their names, addresses, credit card numbers, phone numbers, dates of birth—everything needed to copy their identities.

Believe me, I know what a scumbag I was. But it worked every single time. And we became anyone we wanted. Hey, we were brilliant young entrepreneurs. We had more money than we could ever spend. We partied and did drugs with all the cool people in the city.

But I was emptier than ever. I was certain that if I achieved the things I thought would bring success, I would be happier and more fulfilled. Sadly, I was still me, I still had the same aches in my soul, and I was still a miserable wreck.

Things got worse. I turned to more drinking and drugs. I was lower than low. Night after night I couldn't remember what happened. I became constantly paranoid and believed I was going to die. I attempted suicide. Once, I was sure I actually saw hell. I had several brushes with the law. I was arrested for drug possession and a DWI. I had warrants in several states. I slept with a lot of women I barely knew, including my best friend's girlfriend. I sinned, I sinned, and I sinned. I was a complete and utter waste.

What was I to do? Who could save me from this depression, this polluted life I had created? And I was supposed to be a Christian! A son of God? That was the last thing I felt like. I was betraying God. I was spitting right in His face. I was telling Him to shove it! I had no place else to run. There was no hope for me. This was the end.

WHEN EVERYTHING CHANGES

At my lowest point, I had made friends with some very shady customers around the city. I knew I would soon either have to join them in a full-blown life of crime or flee.

I also knew I needed help. Strange as it sounds, I knew I needed to study the Bible in depth, since it was God's revelation to man.

Maybe it was the prayers of my grandparents, I'll never know. But one day, very suddenly, I decided to choose life and not death. That day, I decided to sell everything, pack up my car, and enroll in Bible college. And that's what I did. I was twenty-two years old, and I knew something radical had to happen for me to really change. If I stayed around the same people and the same environment, I'd die soon. So I fled.

Remarkably, I was accepted to Bible college. It was everything I'd hoped. Not perfect, but just what I needed. For once, I was in an environment of love and care. Within months, I made some good friends. I began to date a Christian girl. I was befriended by a pastor who began to disciple me. That first semester, I was offered a job at his church as junior high director.

I had genuinely straightened out. More so, I was learning to enter into a true relationship with God. I was healing from the pain of abandonment I had experienced as a child, and I was really studying God's Word. I was back on track with the Lord, and my future looked bright.

Until the phone call.

"Tom, this is your attorney."

"Uh, hi. Haven't talked to you in a while. Why are you calling me?"

"Listen, I know you've been doing great and you've really turned your life around. *But . . .*"

Oh no! That dreaded word. I wish that word could be burned from the dictionary. That's the last word you ever want to hear. It could mean anything.

". . . *but* I received a call from the FBI today."

Silence.

"It appears they were following you for quite a while. You need to come to my office this Friday so we can sit down with them and have a talk."

More silence.

"Tom. Tom? Hello?"

"I'm here."

"You're going to have to tell them everything."

"Everything?"

"Everything."

My worst nightmare. My secrets would be revealed. But God wants me to trust Him. He would surely deliver me—wouldn't He?

THE OPEN WINDOW

Sitting in the bathroom in my attorney's office building, I noticed an open window above me. My heart was racing. I had just gone through one round of questioning with FBI agents in the other room. Another round was to come when I went back. Looking at the open window, my only thought was to run.

It was then—of all strange places, in a bathroom stall in Nacogdoches, Texas—that I heard God's voice. All the Voice said was, *Trust Me.*

I washed my hands, went back, and spilled the beans. I told the agents about the counterfeiting, the drugs, the assumed identities, even about the time we created a phony bank. Everything came out. I left nothing hidden. My slate was clean.

A few weeks later I stood before a federal judge, charged with five counts of bank fraud. Each count carried a mandatory minimum sentence. I had already done the math. These were federal charges; there was no such thing as probation. Even though my slate was clean, I still had to pay the price. The *minimum* time I was going to receive was twenty-one years in jail.

Where was God in this?

As the judge read the list of charges against me, he looked at me sternly over his black-rimmed glasses. "It says here you're an upstanding young man who has really turned his life around."

I looked at the floor.

"I believe that," he said. "From the people who've testified on your behalf, and from my own interaction with you, in all my years on the bench, I've never seen such a transformation. So I'm going to help you as much as I can."

Here it comes! I could feel the deliverance. A modern-day miracle in the making. Freedom! I would get off on a technicality and go back to my life.

"*But . . .*" said the judge.

I was really starting to hate that word.

". . . the law will not allow me to dismiss the charges," the judge continued. "So I'm reducing the five counts to the lowest one and giving you the minimum for that. Six months. Three months in a federal penitentiary and three months of home confinement. You'll have a felony on your record, but I know you can overcome it."

The gavel went down. *Bam!*

I was going to jail.

That December 22, everyone else was excited because Christmas was right around the corner. But not me. My grandfather drove his Buick Roadmaster along a winding country road in northeast Texas with me in the passenger's seat. It was cold and miserable outside. Fitting, because that's how I felt on the inside. I saw a sign up ahead: Federal Penitentiary. Texarkana, Texas.

Razor wire. Strip searches. Orange prison clothes. The next three months were a routine of cinderblocks, four people to a cell, roll call, lights out. That Christmas I got an extra scoop of Jell-O for dessert. Jail is all sorts of bizarre stuff. I hate to think about it now. By the grace of God I wasn't subjected to any of the truly horrible things that can happen in jail. Mostly, it was just a bad place to be. Certainly I'd never dreamed as a little boy, "Mommy, when I grow up I want to be a felon!" But I do accept responsibility for being there.

I put myself in prison.

I don't blame my stepfather, or the system, or The Man, or God.

It was me. My own actions put me there.

Prayerfully, thankfully, the grace of God that had begun to work in my life saw me through that dark time in jail. I started a Bible study with my cellmates. We resurrected a chapel service that hadn't taken place for quite a while. We started a choir, of all things—a bunch of convicts singing their hearts out to the Lord. From the depths of those gray walls, we worshipped the God of open windows.

CONFESSIONS OF A GOOD CHRISTIAN GUY

Friends have asked me why I would put all my dirty laundry on paper for the world to read.

The reason? I choose not to lie anymore.

This is me, the real me, continually saved by grace. First Timothy 1:15 says, "Christ Jesus came into the world to save sinners." I'm proof—Public Sinner Number One—of someone who could never have made it apart from God's mercy.

The truth of my story is the most powerful tool I have to dispel lies in my own life. And so is your story. Being honest about my past helps remove the obstacles that hinder authentic relationships with God, self, and others. Sin thrives in darkness. Expose it, and it has no place to run. Force it

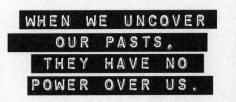

out into the light, and you take away its power. The apostle Paul understood and lived this truth. He confessed that he was the worst of sinners (1 Tim. 1:15). When we uncover our pasts, they have no power over us.

That's exactly what this book is about. Frankly, aren't we all sick and tired of the fake stuff in our lives? Living a lie will eventually separate us from the things that matter most. Living a lie ultimately destroys us, those around us, and the relationships we care about most.

In front of you is an invitation to let Jesus Christ lead you in a good direction. This book is about real men who are closing the gap between who they say they are and who they really are. It's

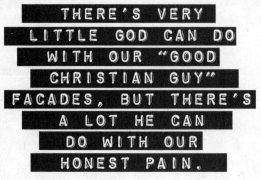

THERE'S VERY LITTLE GOD CAN DO WITH OUR "GOOD CHRISTIAN GUY" FACADES, BUT THERE'S A LOT HE CAN DO WITH OUR HONEST PAIN.

about authentic men who take 100 percent responsibility for the fractures in their souls. It's about being real and being healed.

Why do I write about the dirt in my life? I've learned that there's very little God can do with our "good Christian guy" facades, but there's a lot He can do with our honest pain. If God could help me in my miserable state, He can certainly help you wherever you are. Just the tiniest bit of faith can transform a desperate situation into an opportunity for God's outrageous grace.

With the grace of Christ, you can be free from whatever is a stumbling block in your life. You can change directions. You can live as you were meant to truly live. We need God's grace to truly live. Grace is God's presence and goodness always with us. When we're committing sin, when we're repenting of sin, when we're working ourselves out of the effects of sin—God's grace is always with us. It's never too late. Nothing can remove God's love or forgiveness from our lives. No matter what damage has been done, it's never too late to build or restore. God can restore things in our lives that seem impossible to repair.

A life lived fully begins when we open our hearts to the grace offered us by Jesus Christ. This is a new day. Old things are passed away, and all things become new. You get a new start. Right here, right now.

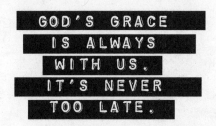

GOD'S GRACE IS ALWAYS WITH US. IT'S NEVER TOO LATE.

REFLECTIONS FOR THOSE WHO CARE
I

TAMMY MALTBY

Galatians 6:2 encourages us to "carry each other's burdens." If someone we care for is struggling with an issue, how can we help him best? How do we encourage him to put away the old and press into the new?

I believe it begins with truly *seeing* another person. I mean really *seeing* him. Entering into his pain, his woundedness, his upside-down world. We must be willing to get our hands dirty in the lives of others. Sometimes situations can feel gray, unsettling, and unsure, but that is exactly what someone did for Tom. Someone entered Tom's world and gave him hope for something more.

How do we become a place of safety for others? We start by being real about our own brokenness and shame, understanding that there but for the grace of God go all of us. Ask questions to draw out your friend. But don't pry. Be willing to let some of your questions go unanswered. Remember, it is the Holy Spirit who ultimately does the work in another's life. Not you. Isn't that a relief!

Everyone has a story that is being written every day. We only see one chapter or page at a time. God sees the whole book:

beginning, middle, and end. He is fully able to work all things together in a person's life to bring forth goodness out of the darkest places. We must release control of how God chooses to do this. We must trust Him with those we love and even with our own pain from the fallout of sinful choices.

Anytime we feel far from God's long arm of grace, we need to know He is close-by. God is in it for the long haul with us. God longs to see us and our loved ones restored and healed. That's been His plan from the beginning.

KEY SCRIPTURE

Now God has us where he wants us, with all the time in this world and the next to shower grace and kindness upon us in Christ Jesus. Saving is all his idea, and all his work. All we do is trust him enough to let him do it. It's God's gift from start to finish! We don't play the major role. If we did, we'd probably go around bragging that we'd done the whole thing! No, we neither make nor save ourselves. God does both the making and saving. He creates each of us by Christ Jesus to join him in the work he does, the good work he has gotten ready for us to do, work we had better be doing. (Eph. 2:7–10 MSG)

WORD OF GRACE

"Too often we underestimate the power of a touch, a smile, a kind word, a listening ear, an honest compliment, or the smallest act of caring, all of which have the potential to turn a life around."

—Leo Buscaglia

CHAPTER 2

"I'VE GOT A DIRTY MIND"
The Never-Ending Struggle of Sexual Sins

When we take a good, hard look at the content of our minds, it can be unsettling.

Imagine with me that someone has asked us to list everything we've thought about in the past twenty-four hours. What would our lists hold?

Or what would happen if somebody turned a spotlight on our sexual history? What if everyone we met suddenly knew the details of everything we had done, or everything that's been done to us?

Even though many of us have followed Christ a long time and deeply desire to obey Him, chances are it's not hard to admit there are aspects of our sexuality we're not proud of.

Make no mistake, I'm talking about myself here. Chances are, I'm talking about you too.

Life can be dirty, even for good Christian guys.

My years of working with men in various ministry situations have convinced me that more of us are sexually wounded than anybody knows. The secrets of our sexual lives lead to a host of problems, including shame, guilt, depression, diseases, lack of self-respect, lack of leadership in church and community, broken marriages, problems with our kids, problems at work, problems with our ministries . . . and in some cases, even death.

Our sexuality is something we need to examine as Christians. God created sex as an incredible gift, something to be a source of joy instead of pain. We were never meant to live in brokenness because of our sexual transgressions. The Lord's invitation to us is to cut away the deadwood in our lives. Christ wants to lead us to the fully alive life we were meant to live.

But . . .

What if everyone knew you slept with your wife before you married her?

Or knew about that one-night stand in Vegas you're trying hard to forget about?

Or about the affair you ended years ago . . . or the one you're tempted to have right now?

Or that you struggle with same-sex attraction?

Or that you frequent porn sites?

Or have a stack of skin magazines under your bed?

Or spend a little too much time thumbing through your wife's Victoria's Secret catalog when it comes in the mail?

Or imagine every woman you see with her clothes off?

Or masturbate compulsively?

What if everyone knew you'd been sexually molested as a child? Or that you did things as a kid with other kids that you knew crossed the line? What if you fantasize sexually about children today? Or about group sex? Or bondage? Or animals? Or about exposing yourself in public?

What if you're single and have never had sex—and sometimes you feel like a second-class citizen as a result?

Or maybe your wife stopped being interested in you sexually years ago. Maybe you keep separate bedrooms and like it that way?

Or you've been rejected and cheated on?

Or you've used your sexuality to manipulate or even abuse others?

What if people knew you think about sex all the time?

What if they knew you can't handle sex
at all?

My point is, sexual brokenness has many facets. We're all sexual beings, and we're all fallen.

Think about the secrets of your life for a minute before we go on—because I'm not writing those things above just to titillate. I want to proclaim from the beginning a reality I've seen at work in the most painful circumstances.

Mark this well. The God who knows the secrets of our inmost hearts also knows the sexual secrets that we feel worst about. The God who knows everything about us knows our sexual wounds.

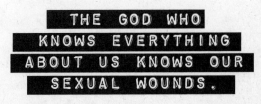

THE GOD WHO KNOWS EVERYTHING ABOUT US KNOWS OUR SEXUAL WOUNDS.

And knowing all this, God's response to us is profound. He loves us more deeply and strongly in the midst of our sin than we ever think possible. And He will shine His light on the path that leads us out of the trap of shame.

This is the God who longs to make us whole. This God longs to straighten out our crooked thinking and twisted desires and fill the empty places that leave us vulnerable to sexual sin. This God offers grace and healing at the depths of our lives. He offers a pathway to self-respect, correction for our bent desires, fulfillment for our yearnings, healing for it all.

But how does this happen? How do we lead lives of victory in the area of our sexuality? Particularly when it seems sexual brokenness is so widespread these days?

EVERY MAN'S SECRET

Consider the following statistics:

- Pornography is a $12 billion business in the United States—bigger than the NFL, NBA, and MLB combined.
- Hollywood releases eleven thousand adult movies annually—more than twenty times mainstream movie production.
- Over 50 percent of evangelical pastors report they viewed pornography last year.
- The number one word used on Internet search engine sites is "sex," according to Alexa Research.
- In a recent survey of more than five hundred Christian men, 90 percent admitted they were feeling disconnected from God because lust, porn, or sexual fantasies had gained a foothold in their lives.[1]

Behind all the statistics is the core issue of lust. Lust is dissatisfaction. We want something more than we currently have.

We aren't satisfied with who we are and what our lives consist of. So we click on to a better sex life, a better woman, a better deal, a better life—the list of dissatisfaction is deep and wide. It comes as no surprise that lust is one of the "big three" temptations mentioned in 1 John 2:16, along with cravings for sin and pride.

When we lust, we hurt ourselves and those we care about. Studies have shown that pornography actually diminishes a person's sexual happiness. People exposed to pornography report less satisfaction with their sexual partner's physical appearance, affection, and sexual performance.[2]

And lust offers us a complete lie—whatever we desire comes to us with none of the challenges of real life. Lust ignores the reality of real people, real pleasure, real happiness, real contentment, real reward, and real success. In the end, all we have left is a false mental image of reality. And that counterfeit existence can destroy us.

There's a further problem with lust: always wanting more. This is not a good type of wanting more, like wanting to achieve something better in our lives. It's the type of wanting more that leads to lust's next step. Instead of just *thinking about* dirty things, we start *acting out* those things.

A number of compelling statistics suggest that pornography has profound social consequences. For example, of the fourteen hundred child sexual molestation cases in Louisville, Kentucky, in a four-year span, pornography was connected with each incident. Extensive interviews with sex offenders (rapists, incest offenders, and child molesters) have uncovered a sizable percentage of offenders who use pornography to arouse themselves prior to and during their assaults. Police officers have seen the impact pornography has had on serial murders. In fact, pornography consumption is one of the most common profile characteristics of serial murders and rapists.[3]

Think it can never happen to us?

How slippery the slope is from thinking to doing. Before long, a thought hooks us. Then an image is burned in our mind. We see it during the day or at work or driving on the freeway. Pretty soon, the thought becomes consuming. And now we can't stop. We're making a phone call. We're stopping at a store we shouldn't. We're booking the hotel room. We're thumbing through the phone book, looking for divorce lawyers. We're calling our wives from a jail cell, having been arrested in a police pornography sting.

That's the dangerous slope a good Christian guy named Andy found himself on.

IT ALL STARTS WITH AN IMAGE

The picture was blurred at first. Then the lines on the TV screen separated enough for Andy to make out a faint image of two bodies. Cable TV had just come in, and Andy was all alone in the house watching the scrambled adult channels.

It seemed innocent enough. Andy was a high school junior, a Christian leader in his school and church. He was heading for Bible college in two years, intent on becoming a worship pastor someday.

I've got to know what's out there, he reasoned, *so I can help my friends who might be struggling with this.*

But a pattern started.

Scrambled cable channels soon seemed like kid stuff. Movies and magazines became more frequent choices. Andy knew his involvement with porn was wrong. Oftentimes months would go by without involvement. Then the Internet hit in the early 1990s. Suddenly Andy had unrestricted pornography available to him all the time. Andy found he couldn't walk away now, even when he wanted to.

Andy remembers the day well. He was sitting in church, now a married man with two young children. He had just come off the platform, having led the congregation in worship—and the split between his two lives overwhelmed him. His job, his reputation, his ministry, his marriage—all were based around leading his congregation into the presence of a holy God, Sunday after Sunday. Andy felt trapped. He knew what had started out as simple curiosity with scrambled cable channels had developed into a massive, habitual pornography problem by then. What would he tell his pastor? His elder board? His friends? His wife?

Another Christian man named Neil has a similar story.

Neil's wedding day was the happiest day in his life. Not only was he marrying the girl of his dreams, but secretly, inwardly, he believed that getting married would solve his long-time problem with lust. Neil was thirty-two when he got married—and technically a virgin. He had messed around with a few girlfriends over the years, but he'd never "gone all the way." Staying "pure" was something he believed good Christian guys need to do. Even then, pornography had always been a secret struggle for Neil. But now that he was married; he could see a naked woman anytime he wanted. Surely this would solve everything, wouldn't it?

In Neil's first year of marriage, he was surprised at how difficult marriage turned out to be. In-laws, finances, expectations, arguments—the problems only seemed to add fuel to the hurt he felt inside. Sex with his wife was surprisingly more difficult than he ever imagined. Pornography and masturbation were always there—familiar antidotes to whatever troubled him.

Neil knew he was on a dangerous path. His wife was amazing—he loved her dearly—but she certainly wasn't flawless like the images of the women he had filled his mind with for years. Neil hated thinking about other women, but it soon became a pattern whenever he made love to his wife. He tried to focus his thoughts, but over time he found his sexual appetite for his wife slipping. Three years into their marriage, a two-month stretch went by without making love once. With tears in her eyes, Neil's wife asked him one evening what she was doing wrong. He seemed so distant from her—so unavailable.

Neil hated himself right then. He hated the person he knew he had become. He told her it was nothing—just stress at work—and he promised to be more attentive to her. But that same night, after his wife had gone to sleep, Neil slipped from under the covers to his den, flipped on his computer, and settled in to his favorite Web site.

Another Christian man, Brian, started out much the same way as Andy and Neil.

As a young adult, Brian landed a job where he traveled a lot for a Christian camping association. Porn channels were available in every hotel room. At first Brian resisted. He'd watch sports or sitcoms—anything—but the temptation was always there.

Whenever he was alone in those hotel rooms, the adult channels called to him, no matter how hard he resisted.

One night, he gave in. He paid the money, watched five minutes of an adult video, masturbated, and turned off the TV. The next morning, it was hard to even look at the charge for the movie on his hotel bill.

But on his next trip, he purchased another video. This time he watched it all the way through.

More trips came. More movies. The bills the next morning were never easy to look at—black-and-white reminders of where he had been. But soon, watching adult videos was a pattern of every business trip he went on. Brian swore he'd never watch them at home. Soon, he found himself longing for the next business trip, just so he could justify watching videos.

It got even worse.

One night, Brian was alone in a hotel room. His meeting that afternoon hadn't gone well, and Brian sought refuge in a six-pack of beer and a bottle of whiskey. About halfway through the bottle, he clicked on a video. Before the video came up, an advertisement for "Swedish massage" came on. Drunk as he was, he still had reservations in his heart: *Wait a minute, I'm a Christian! I'm married and have three kids . . .I can't do this!*

The impulse proved too strong, the effects of alcohol only compounding his lack of resolve. Brian picked up the phone and called the number. When the woman from the "Swedish massage" service knocked on his door, Brian felt his heart pounding like never before. Surely this was way over the line. All he had to do was not answer the door. As the door swung open, Brian remembers the gaudy red lipstick she wore, the sharp pattern of her stockings, her faded faux leopard-skin jacket.

She became the first of many prostitutes Brian slept with over the next four years. The business trips somehow became more frequent. The women became more exotic—and younger. The last woman Brian tried to sleep with he met over the Internet. He thought she was fifteen. She turned out to be twenty-six, a police officer posing as a minor. Only when Brian phoned his wife from jail did the string of lies and deception become revealed.

At one time in his life, Brian had it all—a great job, an incredible family, a loving wife. He ended up divorced, living in a one-room apartment spitting distance from five lanes of freeway. Gone were Brian's reputation, job, career, house, savings, wife, children, and self-respect. He lost it all.

Men, Proverbs 7:26–27 is absolutely correct when it describes the harmful end result of where lust can take us.

> Many are the victims she has brought down;
>> her slain are a mighty throng.
> Her house is a highway to the grave,
>> leading down to the chambers of death.

Whatever the specifics of our sexual sins, the Bible is clear that our sin will destroy us in the end. It's just a matter of time. Scripture is clear that we will always reap what we sow (Gal. 6:7). It's been said we seldom change until the pain of staying the same becomes greater than the pain of changing. What will be the deterrent in our lives that becomes the catalyst for our change?

Will it be the potential of destroying our family?

Or the risk of contracting a sexual disease?

Or the loss of our reputation?

Or our self-respect?

Our job?

Our ministry?

Our future hopes and ambitions?

What is your deterrent? What is mine?

We are not without responsibility in this struggle. Living in grace means we welcome that strange paradox of rest and responsibility. We don't have to clean ourselves up before we turn to God—that's the good news. Christ always welcomes us, no matter where we are and what we've done. But grace never means we lie down on the job—it means, rather, that we quit our attempts to change ourselves by our power. Grace is Christ's leading us in a glorious new direction. Grace is us responding to Christ's call. Even though we might be so wounded that Christ needs to carry us, we are still willing participants in His plan.

With Christ's help, our invitation is to take action now to safeguard our lives and our future. Our call is to take steps to expose the sin in our lives, to seek accountability and boundaries in this area. The answer is not that we stifle our sexuality. It's to embrace our sexuality in the clear, pure way God presents in His Word. Our call is to run toward the God of all true excitement and abundance and life.

That can happen, even in the midst of our sin. It's never too late to turn to God. By His power and might, God transforms our thoughts and hopes and gives us new desires. God heals relationships with people who have been hurt by our sexual sins. God soothes our smudged memories. He replaces our tainted desires for ones that are true, noble, right, and pure.

A miraculous transformation was exactly what happened to Samson. Though much of Samson's life wasn't pretty, God was always there, waiting and willing to welcome him home.

THE GRACE GIVEN TO SAMSON

In Judges 13–16, we find Samson, the strongest man in the Bible. Samson's a real he-man who rips apart lions with his bare hands. A muscle-bound, tough-guy prophet who kills a thousand men with the jawbone of a donkey. If any man could have been physically strong enough, on his own, to resist the lure of sexual temptation, it would have been Samson.

Samson started well. He had absolutely everything going for him. From birth, he was set apart as a Nazirite—his parents dedicated his entire life to God and God alone. Samson grew up with looks, brawn, talent, friends, and ability. He could have led the world in justice if he had set his heart to it.

But much of Samson's life was not lived nobly. In spite of his amazing potential, Samson also had his dark side. Samson's problems started with not being able to control himself. He underestimated the severity of sexual temptation, perhaps thinking that his great physical strength made him invulnerable to sexual weakness.

Samson's downfall was his eyes. He lusted after women—not just any women, but the women of his enemies, the Philistines. Slowly he gave away his power. Samson's lack of self-control allowed his passions to dominate his life. Lust turned to violence and turned to lust again. Samson became a wheedling playboy, an irresponsible womanizer, a man of riddles and tricks and violence. Toward the end of his life, Samson ended up mocked, ridiculed, and blind, his eyes having been gouged out by his enemies. His last official "job" was grinding grain in a Philistine prison. Samson's was a life tragically lived.

But God never gave up on Samson.

And in the midst of his darkest moment, Samson remembered the grace of God.

One night during a drunken Philistine party, Samson's enemies brought him out to jeer at him. In one last burst of uprightness, Samson asked a servant to place him next to the pillars that supported the Philistine temple.

Check out Samson's last prayer in Judges 16:28, paraphrased as follows:

> Oh Lord, just remember me.
> Remember me one last time.
> Just remember me . . . .

With his hands on the pillars, Samson gives one last, mighty, triumphant, righteous heave. The temple walls crackle and shudder. In a flash, the pagan temple crashes to the ground, killing everybody inside—including Samson. In the end, Samson chooses success. He brings one last, poignant, sad but triumphant victory to Israel.

Here's the shocker: fast-forward to Hebrews 11, the great hall of fame of Bible heroes. The people mentioned in this chapter are all commended for their faith—they're called "a great cloud of witnesses" (12:1), people of whom "the world is not worthy" (11:38).

Included in this list is Samson.

Even at the end of Samson's life, after Samson had wallowed in such filth for so many years, even when Samson was broken and wounded—a sightless shell of the great man he had once been—God welcomed Samson back. God allowed Samson to repent, to return, to see the goodness of God and know there is nothing Samson could have ever done that God couldn't forgive.

That's grace.

God considers Samson a hero.

Men, no matter where we are today, this is our invitation. Our call is to make a difference in this world by the grace of God. We're called to help people in incredible ways, to be awesome husbands and fathers, to be role models to our business contacts and communities.

God created us capable of doing all that. He instilled in us the desire to want to do something significant with our lives.

It's easy to miss the mark because we can't deal with our dark issues. Our slide starts with those small temptations we give into when no one's looking. But those small slides quickly turn into downward spirals that zoom us from one dark place to the next. Like Samson, we soon discover that we are not invulnerable to sexual temptation.

It's not that Samson could not have removed some of the deadwood in his life. It's that he *refused* to remove it. He could have gone other routes and chosen different paths. But he chose, by his own will, not to. The deadwood killed the gifts God had given him. Samson destroyed so much of his own potential.

This deadwood is in the life of every man. Call it what you want—bad habits, risky behaviors, wrong choices, sinful vices—deadwood comes from the same evil source, and deadwood is always dangerous. Deadwood keeps us from becoming who we are meant to be. It will overtake us in the end.

But there is hope. Lust does not have to win in our lives. This deadwood can be overcome, and we can move forward to live the abundant lives we were meant to lead.

AROUND THE DEADWOOD

Let's consider some of the patterns in Samson's life and discover how these patterns can relate to our lives today. The following aren't one-stop formulas to an easy, lust-free life. But they are proven principles we can all adapt and fit to our own situations.

START WITH THE EYES

Samson faced the same entry-level problem you and I do—a seeming inability to control his desires. This problem was inflamed by what he saw. All guys are sexually stimulated by sight. It's how we were created, and it's not wrong.

The key for us is to control what comes before our eyes. In Steven Arterburn's foundational book about sexual purity, *Every Man's Battle,* he discusses at length the idea of "bouncing our eyes."[4] Sounds simple, but it's a great place to start. When something even remotely sexually stimulating (in the wrong way) is placed in front of us, we look away. We change the channel. We quickly click off the Web site. We keep our eyes on the road when driving past a billboard. We don't pick up the magazine. We always look women in the eyes—never anywhere else. Men, we've got to start controlling what we look at.

CHOOSE TRUE PLEASURE, NOT REPRESSION

We may think that all pleasure is pleasure, right? But there's a huge difference between real pleasure and substitute pleasure.

Author and theologian Ravi Zacharias explains the difference:

An essential principle in a philosophy of pleasure arises here: all pleasure must be bought at a price. The difference between illegitimate and legitimate pleasure is this: For legitimate pleasure, the price is paid before it is enjoyed. For illegitimate pleasure, the price is paid after it is enjoyed. Turning aside from instant gratification is one of the most difficult things to do. But this is where the battle is often won or lost.

The strength of our will—and this is crucial—surrendered either to God or ourselves—reveals the character we possess, and the strength of our will determines when the price is paid. It is the submission of our will to God that protects us from illicit pleasure, so that we may fully enjoy those which are legitimate. When that distinction is made and honored, life becomes a delight.[5]

Think of choosing real pleasure in these terms. You're trying to lose weight, and you're starving, and there's a piece of cake— a chocolate ganache, triple-layer mousse cake—your favorite! You know if you eat it, it's going to defeat what you're trying to do in your life, but you decide that the pleasure of the moment is worth it. So you eat the cake and fulfill your desire.

Sure, you have pleasure in the moment, but the long-term result is that you're not in shape like you want to be, you're not losing the weight you want, you don't have the energy level you're trying to maintain—and you've broken down your will. The next time, it will be even easier to choose cake over health.

Legitimate pleasure comes when we see the long-term goal. We have a vision of that pleasure, and just because it's available doesn't mean that we immediately indulge in that pleasure. There will come a point when we obtain that pleasure, because we've worked for that pleasure and it's something worth having.

It works both ways. Addictions counselor Elizabeth Crews talks about the idea of fast-forwarding the tapes in our lives. When a moment of temptation strikes, take one minute—one crucial moment—to examine where this action will lead. To false pleasure? Or to lasting pleasure?[6]

So imagine the situation. There you are, feeling hurt, angry, lonely, annoyed, or tired—any of the factors that can weaken our resolves—and temptation is right in front of you. Do you click on the Web site and experience false pleasure? Or do you turn off the computer and go for a walk?

Take a minute to fast-forward the moment. Picture how you'll feel afterward. Picture the loss of self-respect. What will you say—or not say—to your wife about the incident? What if your kids find out? Or your boss? What is the next level of porn you know you'll be involved in soon?

Fast-forward the moment. Whatever the temptation is, it's not as inviting after we consider the consequences. We can see the destruction this type of so-called immediate gratification brings.

Develop Your Accountability System

It is virtually impossible in this day and age to go the road of purity alone. We need a small group of other trusted and godly men in our lives to hold us accountable, to encourage us, to ask us the hard questions that need to be asked.

One of the reasons lust and pornography thrive in the lives of good Christian men is because it remains in darkness. It's a secret that likes to stay hidden, alone, and unexposed where no one can find it. But when we think our secrets are concealed, all we have done is given them power over our lives. The only way to deal with this enemy is to call it what it is.

Meet with men in your church who you know will provide you the support you need. And be a support to them too. Talk it out—*here's what it looks like, here's how it works in my life, and here's what it's doing to me.* You're taking a powerful step of stripping lust of its power. Now it's in the light, where it can be exposed. As long as it remains in the darkness, lust has power, it grows, it takes over.

We have to take responsibility in this area ourselves—to admit that dealing with lust is our responsibility. The degree to which we take responsibility for our lives is the degree to which we will have the power over our lives to change things. For example: if we blame our lust problem on the media, or our family back-ground, or the fact that we were abused

THE DEGREE TO WHICH WE TAKE RESPONSIBILITY FOR OUR LIVES IS THE DEGREE TO WHICH WE WILL HAVE THE POWER OVER OUR LIVES TO CHANGE THINGS.

as a child, or the fact that our wife annoys us, or whatever—we have just given our power away to something else. Something else we can't control and we can't change.

But when we say, *I've got myself in this mess, and I'm responsible, with the Lord's help*—then the path is clearer to a fully alive life. We can take charge and keep the power we need to change.

An Action Plan for Accountability

Let me suggest a few very practical action steps we can all take with the men who hold us accountable, and they with us.

1. Get a piece of paper and take responsibility for the sin issues in your life. Write them down—don't make excuses, but come clean with what you have done. The point here is not to be lurid or sensational, but to not let any secrets reign in your life.

Write out the specific problem something like this:

I have a problem with _____.

It tends to happen mostly when (or because) _____.

2. Fast-forward those issues. If you keep engaging in these behaviors, where will your life be in the next moment? In the next five years? In ten years? Be honest about this, realizing that these issues will get worse, not better.

Write something like:

Whenever this happens, afterward I feel _____.

I know I've hurt _____.

And I know I'm destroying _____.

If this behavior keeps happening like this, it wouldn't surprise
*   me in five years if _____.*

And in ten years, probably _____.

Go over this sheet with your small accountability group or a trusted person in your life. Make this sheet your first step of accountability, and develop your battle plan from there. Perhaps you need to get rid of the Internet in your house or change the location of your computer. Or develop a different commute route home from work. Or cancel your cable or get rid of your satellite dish. Or invest in a computer program that sends a list of every site you visit to your accountability partner. Or develop a plan to immerse your mind in Scripture memory. Or start paying more attention to your wife.

Write something like:
The following steps will help in this area:
I need to ask the Lord's help for _____.
Then take responsibility to _____
by _____
and _____
and _____.
I need to talk to _____
and meet with _____ *every* _____.

When we do this, we're starting to get our lives back—we're taking control, and we are changing. As long as we keep the power in these areas, with God's help we can break this garbage in our lives and be the men God has called us to be.

EVERY AMMUNITION

Men, the issue of what happens in our minds may not change overnight. But the battle for sexual purity can be won with God's help. There is no easy process to overcoming lust, no simple solution that fits every man in every situation. My encouragement for us is to arm ourselves with every ammunition available. The Christian community is beginning to respond much more strongly to this war, and more resources are available every day.

We can do this, now. With God's help, we can take action today toward living sexually pure lives. The great news is this. Sin is sin, and Christ never pretends that sin isn't serious. But Christ isn't interested in exposing our shame; He wants to arm us for victory. Scripture says that Christ was tempted in every way, yet without sin (Heb. 4:15). Jesus knows what we're going through, and He doesn't condemn us.

Christ sees our struggles.

Christ is aware of our failings.

Christ knows our most grievous sin.

Yet He still calls us His friends. And that's the message of amazing grace. The answer to our sexual brokenness is never that we fix ourselves. Yes, we have to take responsibility. But the

CHRIST LONGS FOR US TO TURN TO HIM. THE INVITATION IS ALWAYS OPEN.

answer is always Christ's grace. No matter how many times we fail. No matter what we've done. No matter where we are right now today. Christ is always there for us. Christ longs for us to turn to Him. The invitation is always open.

Jesus Christ is the light of the world. He shines His revealing but healing light on our darkest, most shameful secrets, and His laser love burns out our sexual sins and sexual woundedness and restores us to health. In the end, only a true encounter with the living God will change our hearts.

The invitation is before us. The remedy is to turn to Christ today.

REFLECTIONS FOR THOSE
WHO CARE
2

TAMMY MALTBY

"Living in grace means we welcome that strange paradox of rest and responsibility." I just love that line. Tom totally hit this head-on.

It is true that grace involves *rest*—realizing that we can never do it alone and that we need to lean deeply into the strength and goodness of God. But it also involves *responsibility*—our willingness to take ownership of what we allow to feed our minds and souls.

Do you know someone really struggling with the issue of lust? Let me encourage you to do the following:

1. Give counsel only to people of your own gender. Unless you're married to the person, I do not believe it is wise to address sexual issues with a person of the opposite sex.

2. Bring godly research and knowledge into the situation beyond what you already have. If you are the one who

loves someone who is struggling in this area, be willing to
seek help even at times when he isn't.

3. Be willing to tell your own story. Your story is powerful.
   If you have walked though sexual brokenness, be willing
   to unveil your brokenness to reveal God's faithfulness.
   Secrets can be unbelievably heavy burdens. Sometimes
   telling your burdens helps lift another's.

KEY SCRIPTURE

There's more to sex than mere skin on skin. Sex is as much spiritual mystery as physical fact. As written in Scripture, "The two
become one." Since we want to become spiritually one with the
Master, we must not pursue the kind of sex that avoids commitment and intimacy, leaving us more lonely than ever—the kind
of sex that can never "become one." (1 Cor. 6:16–17 MSG)

WORD OF GRACE

We all have a huge capacity to sin and wander. Yet God is clearly
willing and able to help us all walk through the fallout of sexual
sin—either what you have done or what has been done against
you. Even when we lose it all, God still wants to bring us back to
Him, to restore us, and to give us a future and hope.

CHAPTER 3

"I'M A SELF-MADE MAN"
The Surprising Pervasiveness of Pride

Few of us would readily admit that we have a problem with pride.

Ask me to list the areas of life I struggle with most, and I wouldn't put pride at the top of the list. When I envision people who struggle with pride, I think of performers. Limelight lovers. Dictators, rock stars, professional athletes, or cult leaders—just add red robes, a fleet of Rolls-Royces, and throngs of adoring worshippers. These are high-profile people surrounded by adulation and swagger. Definitely not your average good Christian guys.

Pride rarely seems to be a glaring problem in our lives. In fact, we typically think of pride as something good, don't we? For instance, I'm *proud* when my son does well in soccer. I'm *proud* to be an American. Pride of ownership is something we're encouraged to have when it comes to our houses' curb appeal. For baseball fans, the movie *Pride of the Yankees* is a critically acclaimed classic.

So why does author Harold Warner call pride "the first and most fundamental issue of sin"?

Or why does social critic Josh Ruskin declare that "pride is at the bottom of all great mistakes"?

Or why does theologian Matthew Henry write, "Pride is at the bottom of a great many errors and corruptions, and even of many evil practices, which have a great show and appearance of humility"?[1]

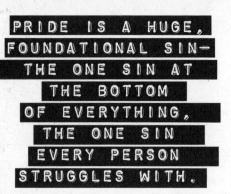

PRIDE IS A HUGE, FOUNDATIONAL SIN— THE ONE SIN AT THE BOTTOM OF EVERYTHING, THE ONE SIN EVERY PERSON STRUGGLES WITH.

Or—most importantly—why does the Bible list pride as one of the three most pervasive sins? In 1 John 2:16, we are told, "For all that is in the world, the lust of the flesh and the lust of the eyes and the boastful pride of life, is not from the Father, but is from the world."

Here's my point. Pride is a huge, foundational sin—the one sin at the bottom of everything, the one sin every person struggles with. Yet having a problem with pride is something few of us readily admit.

Did you catch that? Pride is a huge problem . . . for everyone *except us.*

I don't say that to trap us in a corner. It's just the observation of someone who also journeys down this road of grace.

Maybe pride is more of an issue than we think.

THE PROBLEM UNDERNEATH

Sure, there's a healthy type of pride, like pride in our heritage or pride in our son's baseball team. But pride becomes a problem whenever our attitude about ourselves, our position, our possessions, or our accomplishments goes beyond justifiable self-respect.

The dangerous kind of pride is an elevated attitude of self-importance. It's thinking of ourselves as greater than we are. It's when we start believing we're the ones ultimately responsible for our success. Our chests swell up like balloons, and we take the credit for all the good.

Pride can take forms we might not even be aware of—and this poses one of the greatest challenges for us. It's hard to see the pride in our lives because it often lies underneath the surface of whatever problems we're having.

Take my friend Kai, for example.

Kai is a seminary graduate, a former pastor who now works in Christian publishing. A few days ago he was telling me about some problems he was having in his marriage. "Nothing huge," he said at first. Just a steady slide to a place he and his wife didn't want to be. After nearly a decade of marriage, his wife was growing more distant. Passion had all but dropped out of their physical life. They seemed more like brother and sister than husband and wife.

What his wife really longed for was a weekly date night. She had communicated her needs several times. It sounded simple, but Kai told me he was resistant to the idea. He never outright said no to his wife, but he always found excuses not to take his wife out—he was too busy with work, something good was on TV, the babysitter cost too much . . . whatever.

As Kai and I talked, the real reason came out. "Seems to me she should just love me, without me having to take her out all the time," he said.

Immediately, Kai caught the gravity of his attitude. His pride—his belief that he was *above* needing to take his wife on a simple date—was showing through. Kai had not considered himself a proud person. The sin was noiseless in his life. But Kai's prideful attitude was keeping him from responding to his wife's simple request. Left unchecked, who knows how much damage pride would have done to this marriage?

Think about the various ways pride can crop up in our lives.

Pride can take the form of *entitlement*. This is when we believe we don't need to pay our dues or buckle down and work for things. Or because we've worked for things, a certain type of success should be guaranteed. We deserve it! But when success doesn't come, we blame others or the system.

Pride can take the form of *overconfidence*. Boldness, courage, and daring get pushed too far and become audacious and grandiose. It's when we whisper things like, "I did this all on my own" or "No one around here can do things as well as me" or "Everything always depends on me." It's our attitude and character that are key. How we respond and to whom we give credit make the difference. Do we look at ourselves in the mirror and praise the works of our hands? Or do we give praise to the One who is greater than us?

Pride can also take the attitude of *superiority.* This is when we look down our noses at other people, their possessions, their knowledge, or their behaviors. It's when we say things like, "There's no way I'd hang around with people like that" or "There's no way I'd ever fall to that sin" or "How do people get themselves in such messes?"

Pride can even show up in the form of *false humility.* Ask some people if they have a problem with pride, and they'll say, "Not me; I'm such a loser" or "Pride's not my problem because everything I touch turns to garbage." Even this attitude can be a form of pride because we're weighing our deeds by a faulty scale. We've put our identity in something other than truth. And sometimes the worst arrogance of all is to declare that pride isn't an issue.

Pride can sneak up in the strangest of places. Take a look under the surface of whatever problems you're facing right now. Truly, deeply, in your heart or even out loud, have you ever said anything like:

- I just got a promotion. *All due to my hard work, of course.*
- An investment I made just went through the roof. *Because of my brilliance and financial prowess, my family is sitting pretty.*
- I'm tired of my wife and her nagging. *I deserve someone better.*
- My kid's baseball coach is such a dolt. *I would be a much better coach.*
- My pastor is dead wrong about this issue. *I need to go set him straight.*

- My friend Frank and I both graduated college at the same time, and my house is sure a lot bigger than his. *I wonder what's wrong with him.*
- That cop had no right to pull me over. *I'll give him a piece of my mind.*
- Volunteer to be on the church building committee? *There's no way I'm going to clean gutters.*
- Me accept help? No way! *I'm a self-made man.*
- Me go to a small group? I don't need other guys in my life. *I'm a self-made man.*
- Me be honest with someone? Guys don't talk about their feelings. *I'm a self-made man.*

See a pattern emerging?

It can be a staggering thought when we recognize pride in ourselves. We don't normally categorize ourselves as prideful people. We're good Christian guys. Humility is a virtue we prize.

But peel back the layers, and chances are good that we can see some dangerous attitudes in our lives.

Pride can be at the root of a whole host of problems, including friction with friends and family members, workaholism, burnout, church conflicts, problems with finances, problems with neighbors, problems at work, problems with our children's teachers, even problems with the law.

If left unchecked, pride leads to strife and destruction. It ruins our potential. It makes us unaware of the truth. Pride blinds our reason and our objectivity. It blurs our senses and our ability to make moral decisions. Pride is the beginning of many potential disasters, and it can lead us into all kinds of troubling situations.

Pride was what sparked the fall of Lucifer from heaven and his subsequent transformation into Satan. At one time Lucifer was actually a good guy. He was an exalted angel of heaven—a created being with unlimited potential for good. But pride led Lucifer to challenge God, the ruler of the universe. Maybe we don't go this far in our pride, but chances are, the pride in our lives is prompting us to forget about God. With pride, it's *us* at the center of our lives, not our Creator.

PEEL BACK THE LAYERS, AND CHANCES ARE GOOD THAT WE CAN SEE SOME DANGEROUS ATTITUDES IN OUR LIVES.

Pride can be something we all struggle with, even as good Christian guys. It can give us the appearance of great success at work or at church, it can affirm our ego, and it can make us feel like someone we think we want to be. Then, when we are least expecting it, pride can turn on us and destroy us.

That's exactly what happened to a good Christian guy named Ian. He didn't think he had a struggle with pride. But what happened to Ian almost completely ruined his life.

IAN'S STORY

Ian had been given a lot in life. He was raised in an upper-middle-class Christian family. He went to the right youth groups, camps, and Christian college. His parents instilled in him three family values: pride in yourself, pride in your family, and pride in the work you do.

In Ian's mind, that meant work and image were everything. If anything got in the way, he would sweep it under the carpet. You certainly don't talk about things. And you certainly don't live without the three family values.

As a young man, he married well. Before long, he had two wonderful kids and a job to die for. Things looked good. Ian was proud of all he had accomplished, particularly at an early age.

Life can take a strange twist when all is going well on the surface. It's easy to start feeling like we're responsible for all we've been given. Particularly if there's no room in our lives for failure. Our success makes us less empathetic to imperfection. When our work or our family doesn't quite fit into our definition of success, we start to look elsewhere. That was the beginning of where things started to go wrong for Ian.

To begin with, it took a lot of work to live at the level Ian felt was expected of him. A new car every three years. A nice house in a good neighborhood. Clothes. Boat. Vacations. In his most honest moments, Ian felt like he was trying to live ten years beyond where the family really was. Downsizing simply wasn't an option. They had an image to maintain.

And his wife? Well, she was a great woman—a wonderful homemaker, a vibrant personality, very hospitable—everyone loved her. But she was certainly not flawless. Ian had a recurring fantasy of a former girlfriend he had come close to marrying. The girlfriend had been business-minded. A real go-getter. Ian found himself wondering how his life would be different—better—if he had married her instead.

The final straw came at work. A new boss, a woman, came in, noticed Ian's work record, and began telling him everything he craved hearing: "You're great, you can do anything, and I can't do it without you." Ian started believing it. He and his boss started traveling together. There were expensive client dinners. They would stay out late together. Next thing you know, she sat down at the bar with Ian and whispered, "Do you want to come up to my room?"

In Ian's own words, "I had to prove to myself I could handle any situation, so I could handle this too. The affair I had was all about my pride. It was a way for me to run away from the truth of my life—that I could never be flawless."

Ian remembers the moment his wife asked him to move out when she found out about the affair. Even then, Ian still justified his behavior. Hadn't she pushed him to this?

In *Mere Christianity*, C. S. Lewis called pride "the great sin." He points out that pride is the most serious and lethal sin by far because it's a root sin that leads to a whole host of others, including infidelity and immorality. Pride is what we use to justify violating the bodies of others and our own consciences. *It's our right,* we think.

One long, horrible year passed in Ian's life. He moved to another state and got another job. Then one day in July, a phone call from Ian's wife changed everything. Their daughter had suddenly passed out, her head was swelling, and they didn't know what was wrong. She was being rushed to the hospital.

For Ian, this was the rock-bottom reality he needed. His daughter had always been such a gift. The flight back home was the longest of his life. He remembers the shock of walking into pediatric intensive care at two a.m. and seeing his daughter in a sedated coma with twelve IVs. Her hair was matted with blood because doctors had put a stent in her head to relieve the pressure.

Ian recalls, "I just sat next to her. I didn't sleep for three days. There was nothing I could do. I was totally broken. For once, I knew I was not in control."

Surgeons removed a cyst at the bottom of his daughter's brain tissue. The surgery was successful, and they put her skull back in place.

For Ian, this experience was like coming back to life again. He realized that life would never be perfect, and nothing he did could ever make it be that way. God was in control—Ian wasn't. For the first time, Ian realized that he needed to trust God for everything. Ian's self-sufficiency was shattered—there was nothing he could do to make his daughter well again. He needed to walk in humility every day.

Hours of counseling, confessing, and forgiving followed. Ian moved back in with his wife and family. Today, things are progressing. "I'm amazed by God every day," Ian says, "and purely thankful. I'm not expecting much out of life, just hoping to be used each day. In the way I used to live, pride used to come before everything else—I led my life with pride. God took me and wrecked me completely of that and left me with nothing except Him. And He's enough."

WHEN WE RAISE OUR EYES

There is good news when it comes to pride.

Our Lord knows our weaknesses, even the ones that lie under the surface. Christ knows our failings. He knows how hard it is for us to admit we have faults. How we long for respect. He knows our desires to be competent, to succeed, to be seen as someone who has it all together, even at the expense of truth.

I'm convinced the Lord can take our prideful attitudes and transform us

> **LIVING AN ABUNDANT LIFE IS NOT ABOUT OUR TRYING TO "FIX" OURSELVES BY OUR OWN STRENGTH.**

to be the men we're truly called to be. With Christ, we never have to scrub ourselves up first. We're invited to come to Him in the midst of our failings—in the midst of our arrogance and conceit, no matter if our pride is subtle or overt. We can come to Him when we don't think we're prideful—or when our pride has taken us to rock bottom and laid us flat. Living an abundant life is not about our trying to "fix" ourselves by our own strength. We're not called to heal ourselves, or even to live for Christ by our own power.

All God asks of us is one thing.

THE ONE THING GOD ASKS

This is what happened to Nebuchadnezzar, the great king of Babylon. He started out on the right path, but his success got to his head. God didn't ask the king to figure out how to heal all the harm that eventually came into his life. It was God who healed King Nebuchadnezzar and restored him to greatness. All Nebuchadnezzar needed to do was the one thing God asked.

What was that one thing? Daniel 4 explains in detail King Nebuchadnezzar's critical mistake and the one thing he needed to do.

At the start of his reign in Babylon, Nebuchadnezzar conquered Judah and captured the inhabitants. Babylon became the most powerful nation of the day, and the city's beauty and strength could not be surpassed.

Even though the prophet Daniel had warned King Nebuchadnezzar of the dangers of pride, his warning fell on deaf ears. One day as the king walked on the roof of his royal palace, Nebuchadnezzar reflected on all his accomplishments: "Is not this the great Babylon I have built as the royal residence, by my mighty power and for the glory of my majesty?" (Dan. 4:30).

Notice how pride crept into the king's life. Perhaps it was subtle at first, but now it's overt. There are two key words that led to his downfall: *by* and *for*. These words reveal the king's true heart.

How did Nebuchadnezzar build Babylon? "*By* my mighty power."

For what purpose did Nebuchadnezzar build Babylon? "*For* the glory of my majesty."

Somewhere along the way, Nebuchadnezzar's abilities had gone to his head. He thought he was the powerful one. He believed that all the greatness of Babylon was a result of his intuition, his brilliance, and his might.

Listing our accomplishments is always dangerous. Pride can feel so good. Nebuchadnezzar's statements reveal the essence of pride. *There is none like me! I deserve this, and I love to meditate on the fact that all this was brought into existence solely by my savvy and abilities. And by the way, it's all for me—and dang it, I deserve it!*

The king didn't even get the chance to stop talking before God acted. Scripture tells us what happened next:

> While the word was in the king's mouth, a voice came from heaven, saying, "King Nebuchadnezzar, to you it is declared: sovereignty has been removed from you, and you will be driven away from mankind, and your dwelling place will be with the beasts of the field. You will be given grass to eat like cattle, and seven periods of time will pass over you until you recognize that the Most High is ruler over the realm of mankind and bestows it on whomever He wishes." (Dan. 4:31–32 NASB)

Here's the principle: we are all part of something much bigger than ourselves. We are stewards in a great and mighty kingdom that God Himself rules and reigns over. He gives one of us power to be a king, another the graciousness to be a servant. But whatever position He has given us, we are to serve Him with gratitude and humility. Knowing that God is in control is so important. He is ruler. He gives us life, breath, and success.

Nebuchadnezzar forgot who held the real power. God had given him the position of king for a purpose. It wasn't an accident or chance; Nebuchadnezzar was king because our God put him in that position. But Nebuchadnezzar chose arrogance, even when he had been strongly warned. So God enabled him to see the truth: "the Most High is ruler over the realm of mankind and bestows it on whomever He wishes."

This is sobering and comforting at the same time.

It's so easy to forget who's truly in control. Daily activities, monthly planners, goals, time charts, meetings, planning sessions—

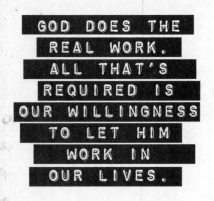

GOD DOES THE REAL WORK. ALL THAT'S REQUIRED IS OUR WILLINGNESS TO LET HIM WORK IN OUR LIVES.

all these can crowd in to help us forget that God is involved in our day-to-day activities. We begin to think our talent, our abilities, our connections are responsible for our success.

Nothing is further from the truth. It's only by God's grace that we can do anything. We are in the positions we're in because God put us there. We have success in our lives because God allows us to. He's in the driver's seat.

So what was the one thing God asked King Nebuchadnezzar to do?

Scripture tells us that the once-great king was literally on his hands and knees in the middle of a field. His fingernails were long and curved under. His hair and beard were wild and unkempt. He had just taken another mouthful of grass. He smelled like a barnyard.

Then he *lifted his eyes toward heaven* (Dan. 4:34).

And immediately Nebuchadnezzar was healed. His sanity

was restored. His honor and splendor were returned to him. He was restored to his throne, and Scripture says he became even greater than before.

The one thing required was Nebuchadnezzar's *willingness to look to God.*

Grace is always available. God is always there. His welcome is always open. Just come to Him. James 4:10 says that when we humble ourselves, God lifts us up. That's grace. God does the real work. All that's required is our willingness to let Him work in our lives. The solution is not for us to try harder at being humble in some vain effort to rid ourselves of pride. Our call is not to try to work our way to a place where we don't need God's mercy anymore.

The abundant life begins when we're honest about our condition.

We need God.

And God's grace is always available for what we need.

PRACTICAL GRACE

Pride keeps us from having close, connected relationships with those who can mean the most to us. Because of pride, we don't want to divulge our inner lives to other men, because we are too proud to admit our wrongs. We don't want to admit our weaknesses for fear they might damage the flawless images we've worked so hard to create. Or we aren't truly honest with our wife, because pride has taught us that the problems in our marriage aren't our fault.

One of the practical ways to deal with pride is to become part of a small group of men who hold you accountable. At first, it may feel uncomfortable to open up your life to other people. Most men are individualists. We're rugged and self-sufficient. We often believe we can do everything on our own and we don't need anyone or anything to tell us different. I admit I've taken pride in myself over the years because I've pulled myself up by my own bootstraps in tough times. After all, it can be hard to ask people for help. It's much easier to say, "I don't need anyone. I can do things myself."

But this attitude of individualism has also kept me from truly being known by those closest to me. Keeping intimacy at arm's length always comes around to hurt me in the end. The Lord continually calls me to be open with a few trusted others.

Having a small group of men to hold us accountable is so important. These are people who really know us. They're friends we can be totally honest with. I'm talking about developing the type of relationships that have no pretense. Just transparency. These relationships often don't come to us. It takes our willingness to step out and ask people to meet with us. Or for us to join a group at our church.

This brings me to another practical way God's grace comes to us.

It's in our nature as men to want to fix things. I'm not talking about the leaky kitchen plumbing; I'm talking about our inner lives. My wife hates it when I try to fix her. She will be pouring out her heart to me about something deep and important, but I cut her off and say something like, "Well, what you should do is . . ." Then the conversation hits a deadend because she's no longer willing to talk.

I don't believe the Lord ever asks us to fix anything. Not ultimately anyway. That's His job. But the Lord does call us to accept responsibility. That can be hard for me to do. It's so much easier to blame someone else. It's easy to allow our pride to run amuck. One bad decision leads to another, our past influences our present, and our pride gets to a place where we don't want help. Next thing we know, we're on such a slippery slope there seems no way back up.

When our pride has led to conflict and strife, God calls us to admit it. *I'm the man, I did it, my actions got us here, I own it.* Ouch! That's painful, but God doesn't call us to be victims or to blame someone else. He calls us to be men of action, men of freedom, men of courage, men of grace.

Truly, the best defense against pride is a good offense. What is the offense? Surrender, plain and simple. Surrender everything we are, everything we have, and everything we will be to the Lord.

When we truly surrender our lives to Someone greater than ourselves, we are not focused on ourselves any longer. We don't have to fight to protect our rights, make our case, or defend ourselves. It's in God's hands. He will lead us, guide us, and bring about the things in our lives that are most important.

Then we get to relax because He's doing the hard stuff!

I encourage us all to take some very practical steps in this area. We may want to begin with a prayer that goes something like this: "God, I give You all that I am today. Every desire, every ambition, every success, every disappointment—they all belong to You. Lead my life today."

We could begin every day with that simple act of surrender. We could take the things that bother us the most and literally give them to God. Let Him worry about those things. I encourage you to stop trying to fix everything and to stop talking to everyone about what's going on. Surrender your situation, let God work it out, and then watch what happens.

You may want to get out your journal and write a few things. Start by writing down the areas in your life where you know pride has a foothold. What are they? How have they taken control of your life? Why have you allowed them to be there?

_____

_____

_____

_____

_____

_____

Then ask the Lord to break the power and the control these prideful issues have in your life. *Lord, I surrender these situations to You freely. I give these away to You. Amen.*

Write out below any additional prayers of surrender.

_____

_____

_____

_____

Then, with a trusted friend, sit down and let him read what you've written. Full disclosure is key. When we bring dark issues into the light, they lose their power.

Finally, if pride has caused you to sin against your wife, girl-friend, or another significant relationship, go to them and ask for forgiveness. Let's get rid of this baggage so it's not weighing us down any longer.

THE PATH AWAY FROM PRIDE

I don't pretend to have it all figured out when it comes to pride. Maybe some of you are saying the same thing. But there is hope.

Through my own process of continually learning about humility, I believe God shows me something of His heart. He's teaching me that honest pain can be healed, but secret pain cannot. When we truly take that truth to heart, we start living in a completely different way—a way that gives life to ourselves and to those around us.

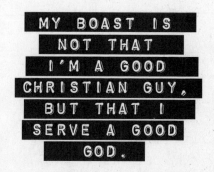

MY BOAST IS NOT THAT I'M A GOOD CHRISTIAN GUY, BUT THAT I SERVE A GOOD GOD.

My bottom-line confession throughout this book is not that I'm lost, but that I keep being found. It's not that I'm straying and messing up with pride, but that I keep being given another chance . . . and another . . . and another.

And my boast is not that I'm a good Christian guy, but that

I serve a good God. I'm growing in His grace—with a *lot* of help—to be the man of God He wants me to be.

That's your invitation too. God's grace is the answer. And we don't journey down this path alone.

REFLECTIONS FOR THOSE WHO CARE
3

T A M M Y   M A L T B Y

God humbled Nebuchadnezzar so he would recognize that 'the Most High is ruler over the realm of mankind and bestows it on whomever He wishes.'" This is sobering and comforting at the same time.

I loved this line . . . did you let it sink in? Read it again: *sobering and comforting at the same time.* That's what the fallout of pride looks like: it's *sobering* when we realize the dreadful consequences, yet *comforting* to know that God is very aware of our prideful nature. In fact, God sent His Son, Jesus, to release us from the bondage of this deadly master, pride.

If someone you care for is struggling with pride, how might you help that person?

When we love people who are painfully prideful, we can choose a higher plane of truth. We don't have to vindicate ourselves, our words, or our ways. When we are attempting to vindicate ourselves, we're really trying to promote ourselves or have things work out in our way, in our time. But if we choose this path, we are working against ourselves.

Scripture tells us, "God opposes the proud but gives grace to the humble" (James 4:6). If someone you care for is proud, draw boundaries, yes, but also resist the urge to fix the person. God will sort things out in His way and His time.

KEY SCRIPTURE

When pride comes, then comes disgrace, but with humility comes wisdom. (Prov. 11:2)

WORD OF GRACE

"The prize with which God rewards our self-abandonment is Himself." —Mother Teresa

CHAPTER 4

"I WANT MORE STUFF"
The Hollow Promise of Materialism

Do you know the feeling?

There you are on Sunday afternoon, watching football on TV—and a commercial comes on. It's loud. It's blaring. And it's for a new truck.

It's not just any new truck. It's the biggest, baddest, toughest truck on the block. It has an engine that blows the doors off the competition, the most rugged frame ever manufactured, and enough cup holders to make nine passengers ecstatic at the drive-through. You need to own one—today!

Not only that, but as you watch the commercial more closely, you notice that this truck promises something more than transportation. It addresses your inner desires. Owning this truck means freedom—you can go where you want when you want. It means respect—people will admire your good sensibility and economic savvy. It means safety and fun for your family—because that's what we men do; we provide.

Bottom line: you *need* this new truck. You *deserve* this new truck. In fact, if you don't buy this truck, something is wrong with you. You're missing out on something incredible. Maybe you're even irresponsible. You're stuck in a rut, confined, and cloistered. You might even be a loser.

When it comes right down to it—*not having this truck means you're not the man you need to be.*

VIVA LAS GADGETS!

I admit it. When advertisements like that come on TV, I have a hard time feeling satisfied with what I've got.

One of my greatest struggles is that I tend to look for inner fulfillment externally. I often believe that material possessions will bring happiness and contentment. My faulty thinking is that the more stuff I have, the more abundant my life will be.

That line of illogic is even stranger considering my role as head of an international orphanage ministry. I regularly travel to countries where people have far fewer material possessions than we do in North America. Compared to the rest of the world, since I have a house, two cars, and eat three times a day, I'm considered wealthy. Yet somehow I still struggle with being satisfied with what I have.

How about you? What kind of pull do material possessions exert on your life? Do you ever find yourself saying things like:

"If I could just make a little bit more money, then life would be great."

"If I could just own a new _____, I'd be happy (or content, or whatever)."

"My buddy just bought the newest _____, so I absolutely need to have one too."

What's dangerous about these statements? The danger is that we whisper them, even though we know the truth.

Think about it. Most churches these days are pretty good about teaching tithing, stewardship, and financial freedom so we can do the Lord's work more effectively. We've heard the messages. We've seen the statistics about debt and giving. We know we need to be financially prudent. We know we need to set a budget and live within our means. We know we need to be vigilant when it comes to consumer spending and give regularly to the Lord's work. We know that the Lord loves a cheerful giver. We know we can't love both God and money. And when it comes to the love of things or possessions, we know we're supposed to follow Christ's teaching in Matthew 6:19–20: "Do not store up for yourselves treasures on earth, where moth and rust destroy, and where thieves break in and steal. But store up for yourselves treasures in heaven, where moth and rust do not destroy, and where thieves do not break in and steal."

We know all that. It's God's truth. And we agree with it. So what's the problem?

The problem is that new PDA. You know, the one that's just out right now. The smallest, sexiest, ultra-coolest PDA ever made. *Slobber. Drool.* And for under two hundred bucks—it could be ours. And wouldn't you know it, by the time this book is published, that new PDA will be yesterday's news. Something is bound to take its place. We'll need that too. Along with the new 109-inch TV. And the new Bluetooth phone. And that new digital video camera. And a new set of golf clubs. And the new widget our next-door neighbor has.

That's the real problem.

The real problem is that material possessions are a lure, no matter how hard we try to convince ourselves they're not. There's Christ's teaching about money and possessions, and then there's what happens in our minds and hearts when we see that new truck commercial on TV. As good Christian guys, we know there's a subtle balance between using money as a tool for good and being sucked into the belief that money and possessions guarantee an abundant life. We know God's blessing isn't about receiving material wealth, yet often when we pray for God to bless us, there's still a subtle hope that God will help us win the lottery. And no matter how many times we gripe about having to clean out the garage, we paradoxically long for more stuff to fill it back up.

There's nothing wrong with material possessions, in and of themselves. The real problem is that, in spite of knowing the truth, we continue to long for fulfillment outside of who we are or what we possess. That becomes a problem when . . .

- *getting stuff* becomes one of our top goals in life;
- *longing for stuff* clouds our minds and shifts our priorities;
- *lack of stuff* causes discontentment and envy, even prompting us to do things we know are wrong.

Where can this all lead? Sometimes nowhere huge, just a mild conflict between what we have and what we want to own. We know something is not quite right in our lives, but we can't put our finger on it.

MATERIALISM, LEFT UNCHECKED, CAN BRING BIG PROBLEMS INTO OUR LIVES.

But sometimes our desire for more things can lead to very harmful places. Materialism, left unchecked, can bring big problems into our lives. My sincere belief about good Christian men who mess up is that they never believed they would actually walk down the road they eventually find themselves on. Their downfalls don't start out as some sinister plot or premeditated plan. The severe slide down just happens. It starts out small—as discontentment, the subtle desire to have more, the looking over the yard at a neighbor's new car.

When I think of discontentment, I think of a good Christian guy named Eric, who confesses he feels envious of the larger house his friend lives in. They went to the same college, earned the same degree, and have followed roughly the same career path. But Eric's friend's wife works outside the house, while Eric's wife stays home with the kids. Eric is happy that he and his wife made that decision, but there are days when he admits it would be nice if his wife was bringing in some cash.

Or Michael, who switched careers in his mid-forties. Just about the time he was hitting some good money in his first career, he had to pay his dues all over again. He knows the Lord led him to switch careers. He's in a much better place. But he can't help feeling a twinge of remorse—even going as far as to doubt God's plan for his life—when he thinks of how costly the switch was. His buddies are all driving new cars. Michael is driving a twelve-year-old beater.

Or Hugh. He's one of those guys who always want to know what something costs. He'll tell you what he paid for stuff and then expect you to do the same. It's a contest. And it's not about who paid less for something; it's about who paid *more*. Whenever Hugh talks with you, the subject always drifts to whatever he owns—lawn mowers, minivans, barbecues, wristwatches, laptops, roofing materials—anything, everything. Somehow he *always* lets you know he's got better stuff.

Maybe you've noticed a pattern emerging in the stories of the men you've read about on these pages. No matter what problems trap us, they all have a common thread: we're looking for external ways to fill internal needs. Conflicts, people problems, addictions, and sins are never just about the problems themselves. The problems reflect the needs we are trying to fill by choosing to participate in vices. Materialism is no different: something external is being used to meet an internal need.

Here's the problem: when we see something we believe we must have, a subtle shift can occur inside our hearts that can lead us astray. It begins with a carrot dangled in front of our face that looks so innocent and appetizing at first. But when we chase the carrot, we find ourselves running around in circles. Quickly enough, we're slaves to a taskmaster we never imagined.

That's exactly what happened to Blaine.

THE RENTAL CAR STRATEGY

Blaine was the picture of a good Christian guy heading for a life-time of success. As a kid, his parents loved him. They taught him strong values. The church was the center of their lives. Nothing could go wrong.

Blaine married, but his relationship with his first wife sur-prisingly turned out to be a disaster. The couple experienced every kind of pain. The marriage ended. One of the side results, as is often the case in divorce, was that both parties suffered financially.

When Blaine married Tiffany, his second wife, he and his daughter were living with his parents in California. Blaine had nothing from a material standpoint, only a dead-end job in a car rental agency. Tiffany seemed way out of his league. She was an attorney, well off, and a top-notch producer at her firm. She excelled at everything in life and was an amazing person. Everything Blaine didn't think he was.

Blaine's confidence suffered another blow when Tiffany received flak from her friends and colleagues for marrying a car rental manager. Everything he owned fit in the back of his Chrysler Sebring. People who knew them wondered if he even loved her—maybe this loser was just preying on this successful woman. The rumors made Blaine feel like dirt.

If only Blaine could earn more money.

His grind began by making a few poor choices. At the time, the choices didn't seem so bad. After all, these choices were "just a little" off track. Certainly not glaring. But every time Blaine had the opportunity to trust God with his finances, he decided to take matters into his own hands.

The idea occurred to Blaine to start falsifying rental return contracts. When a friend needed financial help, Blaine offered to falsify a contract for him. The friend would get money under the table. Blaine would get money too. Nobody would ever know. Besides, he was just doing his friend a favor, wasn't he?

Other "friends" started coming to Blaine for help. Over the next eight months Blaine repeated his scheme, eventually financing more than eighty thousand dollars' worth of bad contracts. Soon, he was bringing in the kind of income his wife was. And he was feeling a strange euphoria he hadn't felt for a long, long time.

Maybe you've done something along the same lines and gotten away with it. It makes you feel so powerful inside for a while—like you've beaten the system. Blaine could write checks and make money magically appear. He could loan money to himself, to his friends, or whomever was in need. He felt like the pillar of his community.

Strangely enough, he was still keeping up the veneer of a good Christian guy. He still attended church every Sunday with his family. He was even still teaching a Bible study. People would come to him afterward and say, "Wow, God really spoke to me through what you said." Blaine would pray for them, close the door, and then go right to his basement to falsify more contracts.

Blaine justified everything in his mind. He even kept meticulous records of every penny he stole in order to pay it back someday when he "got ahead." That was his plan, the plan in his hands, day in and day out. Even down to the day the long arm of the law caught up with him.

Blaine never thought a little white lie on a contract to help out a friend would ever end up like this. He was sentenced to three to twelve years in prison.

One of the things I've noticed about good Christian guys who end up running their boats aground is that they never mean to do it. The *Titanic* didn't mean to hit an iceberg either; but when it did, the whole ship sank.

Getting caught up in sin is not something any of us sets out to do. Losing our families and reputations is never at the top of anybody's priority list. But it's inevitable once we make a habit of compromising in small areas of our lives. Once we take matters into our own hands, the compromises begin small, but soon those small areas grow into molehills, then mountains, and then we're in big trouble.

JUST SMALL COMPROMISES?

Materialism is a symptom of dissatisfaction in our inner lives. That dissatisfaction can prompt us to make a series of small, unhealthy choices that can lead to our demise. At the very least, materialism causes us to be ungrateful for what the Lord has given us right now.

We know God leads us, no matter whatever financial situation we're going through. We know He loves us and wants the best for our lives. But even then, we grasp for something external to fill whatever void is inside of us. We take matters into our own hands. We choose things—not the Lord—to fill our emptiness or to make us feel significant or secure.

This is exactly what happened to King Saul.

Saul's specific problem wasn't how much he owned; it was what he wanted. He wanted to take matters into his own hands. That's dissatisfaction. A series of small choices to do things his way instead of God's way led to his downfall.

Saul started so well. He had everything going for him—favor, stature, and ability. God picked him to be king over all Israel.

In 1 Samuel 13, Saul's dissatisfaction came to a head. The Israelites were being routed by the Philistines. Saul was in trouble. Earlier, the prophet Samuel had told Saul that he would arrive in seven days to offer sacrifices to the Lord and help him. But seven days passed, and Samuel didn't show up.

So Saul took matters into his own hands and made the offerings himself. This was the role of God's prophet Samuel, not Saul's role. As soon as Saul finished, Samuel arrived. What Saul had done sounded innocent enough, but it was a compromise.

Samuel tells Saul,

> That was a fool thing to do. If you had kept the appointment that your God commanded, by now God would have set a firm and lasting foundation under your kingly rule over Israel. As it is, your kingly rule is already falling to pieces. God is out looking for your replacement right now. This time he'll do the choosing. When he finds him, he'll appoint him leader of his

people. And all because you didn't keep your appointment with God! (1 Sam. 13:13–14 MSG)

God gave Saul chance after chance to obey. For some reason, Saul kept refusing. Saul was always thinking that his ways were better than God's. If Saul got into trouble, he didn't trust God to help him; he made his own decision his own way.

In 1 Samuel 15, Saul was told to totally destroy an evil people, the Amalekites. These people were so evil that God commanded Saul to wipe every last trace of them off the face of the earth—including all their possessions. So Saul mustered his army and destroyed the enemy. But he kept the Amalekites' possessions for himself.

After the battle, Samuel arrived and asked Saul if he had done everything the Lord commanded him to do. Saul assured Samuel he had.

"What then is this bleating of sheep in my ears?" Samuel said to Saul (1 Sam. 15:14).

Saul's response is classic: "The soldiers brought them from the Amalekites; they spared the best of the sheep and cattle to sacrifice to the LORD your God, but we destroyed the rest" (v. 15). Saul blames others; he justifies his own actions; he does everything except take responsibility for his sin.

God said to destroy everything, but Saul took the best of the best for himself. This is materialism at its core. A small compromise, but in the end, Saul's small compromises cost him everything.

As men, it's easy to want to take matters into our own hands.

No matter what the reasons for having some sort of dissatisfaction in our lives, we want to trust ourselves, not the Lord. We want to provide a solution for ourselves. We don't want to look to God's best for us.

Materialism is like that. We want something more. We long for fulfillment. We long for peace. We long for freedom, for respect, for all the things men long for.

And acquiring more stuff seems like the answer.

It seems like a small thing to do at first. The logic goes like this: we see something we think we must have. Whatever that thing is promises us something we believe we need. So we buy it, believing that thing will be the answer we're looking for.

That's the lie of materialism.

The lie is that stuff can replace God.

A QUICK-TO-FORGIVE GOD

When you think of all the stories in the Bible that illustrate grace, Saul's isn't the first that comes to mind.

At times, God seems uncharacteristically harsh with Saul. But if we take a deeper look, we can see Saul's choices progressively becoming worse and worse. Saul's sin reaches the point where God has had enough. Sin can be like that. It's not that God ever hates us, but just like Saul lost his kingship, we can lose opportunities in our lives. The more bad choices we make, the easier it becomes to make them. Pretty soon we're doing things we never thought we would.

In 1 Samuel 16:1, God finally declares that He has rejected Saul as king over Israel. That sounds harsh. But think about it. God is the same God yesterday, today, and forever (Heb. 13:8). God is always full of grace, even to Saul. Though God rejects Saul as king, it still takes quite awhile for David to succeed Saul and take the throne. Why the extended time frame? Why didn't God simply make David king when David was first anointed? Or kill Saul right away? In fact, David has the opportunity more than once to kill Saul. But David chooses not to raise his hand against the Lord's anointed—and the Lord blesses David for that.

Could it be that God showed grace to Saul through David? And through time? Saul had lost the position of king, but God hadn't given up on Saul, the man. God could have killed Saul many times, but for whatever reason, Saul's life was spared again and again.

When Saul is finally killed in battle, he's mourned throughout all Israel (2 Sam. 1). David calls Saul the "glory" of Israel, someone who was mighty, loved, and to be grieved (v. 19).

That's grace.

Our small choices may build to the place where we lose everything, but the love of God is always there for us. God is the good Father who runs to meet us when we've returned from the pigsty. We don't have to clean ourselves up first. We don't have to fix our problems. All that's required is our willingness. God invites us to Him with His mercy.

This amazing, unchanging love of God was always available to Saul. It's available to us as well. Apparently, and sadly, Saul never chose to receive it.

I believe the story of Saul could have been so much different.

All Saul needed to do was stop someplace along the way and ask God for forgiveness before his lifestyle went too far. He may not have gotten his kingship back. But his relationship with God would have been restored.

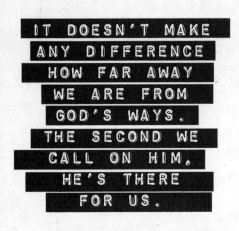

The great thing about God is that the gravity of our sin never matters to Him. It doesn't make any difference how far away we are from God's ways. The second we call on Him, He's there for us.

God is filled with grace and forgiveness for us. Whether we're in deep, terrible sin, or we are sinning in ways we think are insignificant, God is mercy. God is forgiveness.

THE FREEDOM OF FORGIVENESS

As I'm sitting here today, writing this chapter, my seven-year-old son, Gideon, came into my home office to confess something to me. He stole a decorative rock out of a bathroom at Banana Republic.

"Why did you do that, Gideon?" I asked.

"Because I really wanted it," he said, with tears in his eyes.

"Well, how does that make your heart feel?"

"Really bad."

I asked him to go upstairs and tell God what he did and ask for forgiveness.

So off he went, his face buried in his hands, feeling ashamed, up the stairs of our home to his attic. I'm sure he felt not only guilty but even a bit scared. But in his heart, Gideon knows that God is a good God. God is for my son, not against him. He loves him and longs to be with him.

I sat in my office wondering what would happen.

A few minutes later, Gideon barged into my office, tears streaming down his face.

"Did you ask for forgiveness, Gid?" I asked.

"Yes, Daddy. I did."

"And what did God say to you?"

"He said He forgives me!" And out burst another river of tears. But this time his tears were of a different nature; these were tears of joy.

There's a bit of Gideon inside of all of us—someone who strays from the path he knows is true and feels sorry about it. Or even someone who wants something so badly he's willing to make small compromises in an effort to get what he wants.

What do we do when we feel that inner unsettledness?

Some turn to possessions. Having more stuff will make us feel better, won't it?

Some, like Gideon, turn to the Lord.

We have a gracious and compassionate Father who is slow to anger and abounding in loving-kindness. At this point in his life, Gideon doesn't even fully understand the forgiveness of God— he just knows it's available. He was confident that when he brought his sin to God, God wasn't going to pistol-whip him, beat him, or put him down. God wasn't going to be angry and yell at him or reject him.

Gideon knew that his heavenly Father is always ready to forgive, and all he had to do was ask. The very first words out of his mouth when he came and talked to me the second time were about God's forgiveness, because God's forgiveness is one of the greatest wonders available to us.

At the point we stop taking matters into our own hands and put them in God's hands, asking for forgiveness in the areas we come up short, everything changes.

OUR GRACE FOR TODAY

What do we do the next time a commercial comes on TV and we're positive we must have whatever's being shown to us?

Before we run out and buy something, I encourage us to take a look at our inner lives. What is the dissatisfaction we're feeling? Why do we think we must have this item? What are we convinced this item will do for us if we buy it?

Run through a short checklist: what kind of small compromises might we make if we buy this item?

- Will it strain our family budget?
- Are we getting it simply because we know it will provoke envy in our friends or neighbors?
- If we buy it, do we believe our status will somehow be elevated or improved?

Bottom line: are we turning to possessions as the solution to our lives, and not to God?

Here's something very practical you can do in this area. Take a moment to think through what you own and what you want to buy, and write these in your journal. Ask the Lord to help you prioritize your needs and wants—to show you what you truly need and what will bring Him glory. Then talk about this issue with a trusted friend.

> ARE WE TURNING TO POSSESSIONS AS THE SOLUTION TO OUR LIVES, AND NOT TO GOD?

And, of course, turn to the Lord. Pray.

If you are struggling in this area, I encourage you to follow Christ no matter where you are. I have found that during hard times in my life, I don't know what to say to God. How do I pray? How do I ask for forgiveness? Where do I start? I have found much comfort and truth in the ancient prayers of the church. These prayers, which have been offered to God for hundreds of years, can be a springboard into prayers from our heart. This is a safe place to begin with God, and He'll take it from there.

Here are the words to an old prayer you can pray anytime, day or night. This simple prayer addresses our true needs before the Lord. Grace is always available to us. Grace is the answer, as found in Jesus Christ.

Will you pray it with me now?

Almighty and most merciful Father,
We have erred and strayed from thy ways like lost sheep.

We have followed too much the devices and desires of our
own hearts.

We have offended against thy holy laws.

We have left undone those things which we ought to
have done;

And we have done those things which we ought not to
have done;

And there is no health in us.

But thou, O Lord, have mercy upon us, miserable
offenders.

Spare thou, O God, those who confess their faults.

Restore thou those who are penitent;

According to thy promises declared unto mankind
In Christ Jesus our Lord.

And grant, O most merciful Father, for His sake;

That we may hereafter live a godly, righteous,
and sober life,

To the glory of thy holy Name. Amen.[1]

REFLECTIONS FOR THOSE WHO CARE
4

TAMMY MALTBY

God has a tender heart for prisoners—and we all have a prison of some sort. If we live for anything other than honesty, truth, and love, we become imprisoned to that thing: money, lust, discontent, riches—you name it. Materialism and living in a prison go hand in hand.

Strangely, while bad choices do have a consequence, prison can become a holy place. When we are stripped of our pride and personal choices, the Holy Spirit tenderly works to repair our bruised souls.

Blaine told me recently that God is the owner of his reputation now. He no longer carries any secrets. It has taken him years to live clean and honest. There is no room in his life for anything but complete disclosure. Though it can make people uneasy, he has learned painfully this is the only way to really live free. And free he is. And by God's grace, free he will stay.

Blaine's complete brokenness has made him an amazing man of God. To be honest, I don't think I would have liked him much if I had met him years ago. He would have been a lot more zipped up, of course; he would have looked a lot cleaner. He would have fit better into most of the churches I know. But there would not have been the profound beauty in the brokenness I experienced in him today. That brokenness, strangely enough, is completing . . . engaging. Quite frankly, I forgot I was talking to a man who was once in prison. It felt like I was talking to Jesus.

Where do you most want to be? A place where your relationship with God and others is at peace? A place that brings eternal joy and contentment? A place of transparent freedom and life?

Getting to that place will cost you something: a broken and poured-out life.

Nothing outside of honest brokenness before Jesus will bring you life. True life is a free life, a life that celebrates simplicity. It is a life that invests in things where moths and rust cannot destroy and thieves cannot break in and steal.

KEY SCRIPTURE

It's obvious, isn't it? The place where your treasure is, is the place you will most want to be, and end up being. (Matt 6:21 MSG)

WORD OF GRACE

True life only comes in authentic living and simplicity. As God's Word so clearly states, "Godliness with contentment is great gain" (1 Tim. 6:6). Even if you're in prison—and we all have prisons of some sort—this is a gain that can produce beautiful, intoxicating freedom.

CHAPTER 5

"I NEED MY DAD"
The Confusion of Parenting and Pain of a Father-Wound

I need my dad."

What's so confessional about that?

It's not like we're struggling with something harmful like, "I've got a dirty mind."

Yet the statement "I need my dad" is something all of us good Christian guys confess to some degree whether we realize it or not—and its implications go further than we might think. When we were young, we needed our fathers to be there for our security, guidance, and confidence. Now that we're men, we need our fathers for their wisdom, support, and camaraderie.

Don't believe me? Try this out for size. A few years back, there was a scene from the sitcom *Friends* where Joey has taken Rachel out for a date, and they're comparing pickup lines. Joey's are all overt, like [deep voice, Italian accent] "How *you* doin'?"

But Rachel's are more subtle. She takes Joey's hand and says, "Tell me about your father."

Tough-guy Joey doesn't realize it at first, but he quickly begins to unload his soul.

So do a little experiment of your own. The point of this is not to get all mushy on each other, but next time you're sitting down with a friend, ask him to tell you about his father while growing up.

What you'll see firsthand is that every man has a story to tell about his father, and often he's more wrapped up in that story than he realizes.

Typically, you'll get one of three responses from your friend:

1. His father was strict and controlling, sort of like a drill-sergeant.
2. His father was nurturing, caring, aware, and involved.
3. His father was passive or absent, with little or no involvement in his life.

Or maybe some combination of these three.

Our fathers are integral parts of our lives. We can't separate who we are today from our father's influence on us. Dad will always be there to some degree. We get our ideas of what it means to be a man (or what it doesn't mean) from our dads. Dads affect how we talk and think, what kind of profession we have, what kinds of activities we are or aren't involved in, how we treat our wife, how we parent our children, and much more.

Dads are part of who we are. They are our heritage and our biology. Whatever diseases they contracted, we are more likely to come down with. What we say to the checkout clerk, how we handle money, what sort of car we drive—all hearken back to our fathers. Fatherhood is one of the core issues in how we see and trust God. How our fathers raised us affects our temperament. We may be nervous or angry or carefree or hard-driving. Without a doubt, our fathers had a hand in shaping who we are.

Think of it this way. Children from fatherless homes are:

- Five times more likely to commit suicide.
- Thirty-two times more likely to run away.
- Twenty times more likely to have behavioral disorders.
- Fourteen times more likely to commit rape.
- Nine times more likely to drop out of high school.
- Ten times more likely to abuse chemical substances.
- Nine times more likely to end up in a state-operated institution.
- Twenty times more likely to end up in prison.[1]

Fathers affect us all.

And we need our fathers.

How about you? If someone asked you to talk about your father, where would you begin? How would you describe him? What kind of reaction does he cause in your life now? How has he affected who you are today?

Would you say your father was the greatest guy on earth? A real Bill Cosby all decked out in funky sweaters and eating pudding?

Or was he Dagwood Bumstead, sneaking off every chance he got for a nap on the sofa?

Or Archie Bunker, yelling at the neighbors and blowing raspberries at anyone who disagrees with him?

Or Clint Eastwood, a real man's man?

Or frightening and horrid, like Hannibal in *Silence of the Lambs*?

Or maybe he was just a regular guy who loved your mom and paid his taxes and had his share of strengths and weaknesses like most of us.

Whatever type of dad you had—good, bad, indifferent, wonderful, absent, or anything in between—he left his mark on you.

And there's one foundational issue that affects your relationship with him today. The problem is simple:

Your dad was a sinner.

No matter what type of dad you had, he was imperfect. Even if he was the most wonderful man in the world, he still made mistakes. Just like we make mistakes with our own children. We can't escape that fact. And that colors how we see the world.

Perhaps nowhere do we see this coloration more than when we become parents ourselves. When we first hold our infant son or daughter, without a doubt, the way we parent from that moment on means we must confront the mistakes our fathers made with us. We are fathers now, and how we learned to be a father is inseparably linked to the parenting (or lack of parenting) we received from our dads.

So maybe the confession for this chapter is actually twofold: "I need my dad" and "I have questions about parenting." Because parenting is full of challenges. And the fathering we received and the fathers we become are closely intertwined.

The invitation for us as men is always to be the men of God

we're called to be. Part of that means sifting through mistakes. We're not called to blame our dads or hate them (even if they were horrible). The point is that the mistakes of our fathers affect us, and we need to figure out the harm and the benefit in our own lives today.

We're always called to be responsible for our actions, no matter what sort of influences lead us to take those actions. Our call is to be the men and the fathers we need to be.

That call is seldom easy, but it leads to a place of wonderful opportunity to lead the lives God calls us to.

Being a true father. Being a true man. It's part of the abundant life God has for us.

Ready to do a little work? Let's explore some of the issues surrounding fatherhood.

GOOD DAD/POOR DAD

There are moments when I wonder if I'm doing the right thing with my kids. I think all of us as fathers wonder this from time to time.

Being a father is a great joy, but it can also be a ton of work. We wonder if we're making the grade. We wonder if we're instilling the kind of values in our kids we know they need to have.

What are some of the mistakes in this area? Maybe these patterns were ingrained in us from our own dads. We see them, struggle against them, but try as we might, we can't seem to escape them. What do we do?

- We wonder if we're letting our wife be the parent. She seems so much better at this parenting stuff than we are. It's a lot easier to come home from work, grab the paper, and zone out for the rest of the night.

- Maybe we're concerned that we want to be best buddies with our kids. We know they need discipline, but our aim is to have them *like* us. And if we disciplined our kids, they would hate us, wouldn't they?

- Maybe we try to buy our kids' love. When we walk into a store with our kids, it becomes Christmas no matter what day of the year. Our goal is to make our kids happy—we love doing it. And the more stuff we give them, the happier they'll be. Right?

- Perhaps we are heavy-handed fathers—we yell all the time or become physically abusive. Boy, that kid of ours can drive us up the wall!

- Maybe we're passive or disinterested fathers, letting our kids run the show. *Going out to a party, honey? No, no curfew, no questions about who'll be there—just have fun!*

- Some of us are single dads—we only get to see our kids on weekends and holidays. Our kids share a different roof than ours. Part of the time they're parented by a stepdad. We wonder if the amount of contact we have with them will ever be enough.

So where do we learn the skills to become the kind of father we desire to be? We can't get around this fact: one of the key places our parenting skills (or lack of skills) come from is our dad.

It's funny. Do you ever remember saying when you were young, "When I'm a dad, I'll never do that to my kid"? And then you grow up and have kids and do the exact same thing! Our fathers can have an effect on us far stronger than we realize.

Call this a mark, or an icon. All men have a mark that was given to us by our fathers. For many of us, this mark is mostly a positive thing—we have a real example of what it means to follow the Lord wholeheartedly,

ONE OF THE KEY PLACES OUR PARENTING SKILLS (OR LACK OF SKILLS) COME FROM IS OUR DAD.

even though our father wasn't perfect.

But for many other men, this mark is a definite wound—a father-wound—a role our fathers were supposed to fill but didn't. Now that mark has become a missing piece of our hearts that we try to fill for years to come.

Writer and minister Frederick Buechner knows this mark all too well. His father committed suicide when he was a young boy, leaving a gaping father-wound in his life. He writes of the push-pull paradox many of us feel toward our fathers. We know that something is missing in our lives, a void we desperately want to fill. But we're not sure how to go about it. We can ignore it, pretend it's not there, hope it will go away—none of that seems to work.

In *The Magnificent Defeat,* Buechner writes:

It is a peculiarly twentieth-century story, and is almost too awful to tell, about a boy of 12 or 13 who, in a fit of crazy anger and depression, got hold of a gun somewhere and fired it at his father, who died not right away but soon afterward. When the authorities asked the boy why he had done it, he said that it was because he could not stand his father, because his father demanded too much of him, because he hated his father. And then later on, after he had been placed in a house of detention, a guard was walking down the corridor late one night when he heard sounds from the boy's room, and he stopped to listen. The words he heard the boy sobbing out in the dark were, "I want my father, I want my father."[2]

What's the confession in the statement above?

"I need my dad."

Here's the paradox: we're drawn to our fathers, but our fathers are imperfect. Some sort of father-mark is in all of us. And for as many fathers as there are, there are that many experiences we have with them. Nobody falls into definitive categories or labels. What we do have in common is that we all have had fathers and our experience with them has left a mark on us.

For some of us, it's a mark of strength, even though our fathers have been imperfect. We have fathers who encourage us, pray for us, and continue to instill in us a strong level of confidence.

For many of us, that mark is a painful bruise of hurt and disappointment.

That's how it was in my life.

And by the grace of God I'm praying never to make the same mistakes my father made with me.

MY FATHER-WOUND

The issue of fatherhood is very personal to me. To begin with, I've chosen to address the issue of fatherlessness as my profession. As head of an international orphanage ministry, it's what my life and ministry are based on. Being a father to the fatherless is my passion, my calling, and my life's work.

This issue is personal for another reason. If there is one thing I'm afraid of more than almost anything else, it's failing as a father. You see, my wife, Emily, and I have six kids. Yep. You heard right. Five are our children by birth. One we adopted from Russia.

And quite frankly, I have good reason to fear failing as a dad. I know firsthand what it feels like to be fatherless. I know how much pain and confusion can come into a person's life when his father messes up, or doesn't even show up for that matter.

I didn't meet my biological dad until I was twelve years old. We tried to meet once. Or rather, he tried, I guess. The earliest memory I have of a father was when I was five. My mom and I were living with my grandparents in Thousand Oaks, California. I had no recollection of what my dad looked like; no memory of the sound of his voice; no understanding of his ways, his passions, or desires; no knowledge of the man who fathered me and gave me life.

But I longed for my dad! It was my confession then, and it's still true today. And not knowing him then only made me wonder and long for the hero he must be.

I remember the incredible excitement I felt when my grandpa told me that my dad was coming to visit me. I could hardly contain myself. As the hour of his arrival approached, I made a little snack bag for myself, got all dressed up, and ran to sit on the curb in front of the house to wait for my dad. Grandpa said we still had half an hour until he was coming. I sat, and I paced, and sat, and paced, all the time eagerly looking down the street for my dad's car.

Nothing.

After a while, my grandpa came out, his face grave. "I don't think your dad is going to be able to make it this time," he said.

I kept looking, craning my neck to look down the road. "But he promised," I said. "Can't we wait another five minutes—just five minutes—*please*!"

Grandpa nodded, and we stood another five minutes.

Then another ten minutes.

Then another fifteen.

All the excitement I had felt that morning drained from me.

When at last I realized he was not coming, I began to weep. Grandpa picked me up in his arms and carried me inside.

I wish I could say that was the only painful memory I ever had about a father. But it wasn't. Two years later, when I was seven, my mother married someone else.

My stepfather was a military man, hard disciplined, alcoholic, and abusive. One evening shortly into the marriage, Mom and I drove home to see him passed out cold on our front porch in his Navy whites. Both of us wondered what to do. Maybe we could just sneak past him and get inside. If we tried to wake him, he'd hit us—we had already both experienced that.

During the next nine years before she finally divorced him, my mother tried to leave my stepfather seven times. For some reason, she always ended up coming back. There were always promises of love. Promises that things would be different.

But soon the hitting would start again. For both her and me. That was the way it was until I was fifteen—a life with a dad who was full of empty words, empty actions, and an empty heart.

Two fathers. Both sinners. That's what I live with today.

EMILY'S FATHER-WOUND

There's one final reason this issue drives home for me. It's my wife Emily's story.

To meet my wife today, you'd never know she's been through some astonishing horror in her life. I won't tell her story in depth here; I'll just give you enough of a flavor for it to know where she's come from.

Emily grew up in a cult, a bizarre offshoot of Mormonism that allowed and encouraged polygamy. As her father rose in the cult, her grandfather encouraged him to take another wife, but Emily's father rebelled and fled with his family.

For several years the family was on the run. There had been rumors of extreme acts of vengeance on behalf of the cult. Finally, Emily's family settled in Texas. But their security was short-lived. Cult members found the family and shot Emily's father, along with a brother, an uncle, and a niece. Emily was twelve when her father was murdered.

Emily's mother entered the witness protection program, along with all the children in the family (Emily has five brothers and sisters). The fear was unbelievable. They always needed to watch out for who might be looking for them. Finally the mother snapped, and she ended up in a mental hospital being treated for severe depression.

When Emily's mother got out of the hospital, nothing was quite right again. One Saturday morning, thirteen-year-old Emily was just getting up for a basketball game when she heard a gun go off. Her mother had shot herself in the head, leaving her six children orphaned.

The one bright piece to the story is that Emily and her brothers and sisters had been saved through the ministry of a Christian church and went to the church's school. One of the teachers at the school took in all six children and raised them together.

Emily and I married when she was twenty and I was twenty-five. Two years later we adopted an eleven-year-old orphan from Russia. Emily pushed strongly for it—through the years, the pain in her life has been transformed to compassion. She knows firsthand what it's like to not have parents, and she decided to devote her life to being a parent to the parentless.

THE GRACE TO PARENT WELL

So that's us, the Tom Davis family. Emily and I had horrible role models from our biological families, yet we've chosen to create a solid family with six children of our own. And as a profession, being involved with fatherless children is something we do on a daily basis.

Emily and I still struggle with trust and fear issues today, which affect our marriage. We continually work to come to grips with abandonment and pain issues. The sin done against us sometimes causes us to act out in sin against someone else.

But something we've learned, and we keep learning, is that we aren't doomed to be the type of parents we had. We have a choice in the matter. We can choose to be passive, abusive, or abandoning parents, or we can decide to press into our children's lives with goodness and grace.

Where do we find the power and modeling to do that? From God, our perfect Father. He will never leave us.

Through God's grace in our lives, Emily and I have made the choice to be active and aware parents to our own six children. When we do make mistakes (and believe me, we do), there is always grace in our lives. God will always seek us out. God continually reaches out to us. God heals the father-wounds in our lives and gives us the hope we need to continue.

This helps us be the parents we need to be.

This grace is available to all of us. We're all nursing some sort of father-wound. Even if we had the best dad, he still made mistakes. And we've got to sort through those mistakes. Even if our commitment is to be the best dad we can be today, we'll still make mistakes with our own children.

Sure, we can attend parenting seminars and sort through our own past lives. Sometimes, the best therapy and healing might just come from being out on a long hike somewhere or from building the perfect model airplane with our kids.

The task is not that we try harder or do more. It's that we realize our confession: "I need a dad." And we turn to our heavenly Father, a perfect Father. He is always there for us. And in Him we find what we need.

A good Christian guy named Brant experienced this grace. When he told Tammy and me this story as we researched this book, he wept openly—and I do mean wept—head in his hands, sobbing. The abandonment and fear issues he felt as a young man are things he deals with today. His story is one of profound emotional abandonment. And where it took him nearly cost him everything.

BRANT'S STORY

From as far back as Brant could remember, there was always church, stained glass, potlucks, and sermons. Brant had a bellyful of church while growing up. His parents were committed to Christian service, and their lives revolved around church activities.

On the outside, everything looked pristine.

But a boy needs more than a show of Christianity. Brant's father never served in that role. Brant's earliest memories were a father who was always involved in something other than him.

In his early teens, Brant did what many young boys do in his position—he took the other road, rebelling against everything his father supposedly stood for. Church, family, whatever it was—Brant went the opposite direction. Even the negative attention from his dad seemed better than no attention at all.

But the flares Brant was shooting up to his father didn't register. His father either didn't care or wasn't paying attention.

So Brant tried both extremes—anything to get a response from his dad. For some time, he excelled in school, shone on sports teams, whatever he could do. Still no response.

Strangely, the only thing that seemed to garner a nod from his dad was when Brant started to get interested in girls. A girlfriend came along in junior high, and Brant's dad regularly offered to drive him over to her house. Finally he was getting some affirmation. Brant and his girlfriend were left alone for hours at a time, so they experimented sexually. "Go get 'em, Tiger!" his dad said, when he found out.

But there was no fatherly protection, no guidance, no loving rebuke or wisdom. Just abandonment.

This wound with his father continued to grow over his life and into young adulthood. Once, his dad had a plan to start a Christian backpacking ministry. At the same time, Brant was moving to a new city to begin a job. Brant, still quite young and inexperienced in business and housing matters, asked his father for help in finding a good place to live. His father rushed around and put him in an apartment in the worst part of the city.

"He was in such a hurry to get to his new ministry he didn't want to bother," Brant said.

But it was tougher than that. With his new (horrible) apartment secured, Brant's dad laid down the law: "Don't call me, and don't ask me for any money," his dad told him. "You're on your own now. Be a man." Then his father got in his car and took off for his new ministry.

Be a man?

Brant had no idea how to be a man.

That first night in his new apartment, Brant heard screaming and shouting outside. He opened his window and watched the police chase a man. When the man ran into the open, they shot and killed him.

"I was so scared," Brant says of the experience. "I desperately wanted to call my dad, but he had told me to leave him alone. I didn't know what to do."

Again, it's that push-pull paradox exemplified by the confession, "I need my dad." We're drawn to our fathers, but our fathers are imperfect. So what did Brant do?

The only place Brant had ever found comfort was with women. The first night in his apartment, he called his girlfriend in Chicago, looking for solace. This further ingrained his pattern of going to women to find strength and affirmation as a man.

Within a few years, Brant was more established and started making a bit of money. Having little identity of his own, he found it in partying. Another girl came into his life, a cocaine addict. She invited him to join her. Since he had established a pattern of looking to women to feel like a man, he did. Shooting cocaine soon led to dealing cocaine. Soon he found out he was infected with hepatitis C, the type for which there is no cure.

Brant continued on. He was a Christian, and still went to church. In fact, he met his wife, Jen, at a singles' group at church. But marriage did not cure Brant of his addictions. The only solace he had ever felt was when he was with women—this meant more than one.

When his wife was pregnant with their first son, Brant began to feel like life was out of control. A softball game, an after-work party, and a few drinks later, he was in bed with another woman. His first affair. Holding his newborn son at the hospital, Brant silently promised him he would never, ever, do that again.

But less than two months later, he had another affair.

Then another.

And another.

And another.

The secret seemed safe. Years went by, and the couple had more children together. On the outside, everything looked good. Brant had a successful job. They owned a lot of stuff. Their children were beautiful. The perfect Christian family.

Brant realized he had acquired a very important skill to pull off this kind of duplicity: compartmentalization. Any part of life could be placed in a compartment, safe and sheltered, untouched from other areas of life—women, drugs, marriage, church, God. He convinced himself he could go to church on Sunday and feel the presence of God and feel great about himself. One compartment. Then he would do whatever he wanted the next day. Another compartment. And never feeling guilt.

Brant's wife had her suspicions. Problems led to counseling. Brant went by himself and didn't tell his wife all that was happening in the sessions. He was diagnosed as an opportunist sex addict—meaning, if a woman was responding to him in any way, he would try to conquer her sexually. The secret was still safe with him.

Or so he thought.

One day, a letter arrived in the mailbox addressed to his wife.

Dear Jen,
Your husband has been having affairs with multiple women behind your back. You need to know this. I can prove it.

> *Signed,*
> *Someone who cares*

Brant's secret was out. His life was built on a bed of red-hot lies. The mark was seared into his psyche—Brant's dad didn't know how to love him, and now years later, Brant had no clue how to love anyone else. His affairs were all about a desire to not be abandoned. He even thought the love was real. He would spend hours afterward cuddling with his one-night stands, pretending he was loved and fantasizing that the security he craved would never go away.

A few years ago, Brant confronted his father about a variety of situations while growing up where his dad was absent.

"All those times, where the hell were you?" Brant asked.

"What do you mean?" his father said.

"As a father, you were never there. You never protected me. I'm a father now. I know my kids, I know their hearts. You never knew mine."

Brant's father just stared at him. "I have no idea what you're talking about," he said.

Brant was prompted to probe deeper. He asked his father what kind of father *his* father (Brant's grandfather) had been to him.

This was the breaking point. Brant's dad began to cry. "My father never—ever—loved me," he said.

As one generation goes, so does the next . . .

For Brant, the anonymous letter was the beginning of his end.

His wife confronted him. His secret was out, and it came dangerously close to destroying everything that was important to him.

Fortunately, Brant was able to come to his senses. He says now that each day—even when he was so involved with his sin—his Father God was scanning the horizon, looking for him, calling out to him, seeking to find him however lost he was. And God never gave up on Brant. God never let go of His passionate grip to find him and bring him home again. With the help of a group of trusted friends, the strong support of his wife, and a system of accountability built into place, Brant was able to progress toward healing and wholeness.

Today, his marriage and family are stronger than ever. But this time it's a true strength, one built on honesty and openness, not on lies and deception.

There's an invitation in that for all of us. When we get to be adults, there is no one-step formula in terms of how we are affected by our fathers.

The only certainty is that we *are* affected.

No matter how we respond to that, even if we turn to a life

of rebellion and pain, God is still waiting for us, scanning the horizon, welcoming us home.

It doesn't matter if you're an average guy or if you're a king. God is still the same God of grace.

THE HOLE IN KING DAVID'S HEART

In many ways, King David was a good man. He led the armies of Israel. He was called a friend of God. He was the most powerful man of his time. The lineage of Christ flows through David.

But just like us, David had issues in his life that caused him difficulties and heartaches.

We can only speculate what kind of a father David had. His name was Jesse, and David was the youngest of his sons. The Bible doesn't tell us a lot about Jesse's parenting abilities, but we do have one glimpse into how Jesse viewed David as a son.

In 1 Samuel 16, God sent the prophet Samuel to the house of Jesse to look for a new king. Of course, Jesse had his own idea of which one of his sons should fill this role. Jesse paraded all seven of his older sons in front of Samuel but didn't seem to give a second thought about his youngest, David, who was out in a field somewhere taking care of sheep.

To give Jesse the benefit of the doubt, perhaps he never mentioned David to Samuel simply because David was the youngest and not yet a man—certainly someone Jesse never imagined a king would look like.

But I don't really buy that.

Samuel finally asked Jesse, "Are these all your sons?"

And Jesse said something akin to, "Well, no, I have one other son, but he's kind of the runt. You really don't want him."

This statement probably drifted back to David. At other times in Scripture, David's brothers demonstrated an insensitivity and callousness to him. How do you think David felt when he caught wind of the remark? His father showed off all his other brothers, but not him. Did that help him feel more masculine? Did that give him any confidence or identity as one of the sons of Jesse?

I don't think so. If that were my father saying that about me, this is what I would hear: "You're no good. You could never be king. God would never choose you. Go back into the field where you belong, because you're no better than a shepherd boy, and that's all you'll ever amount to!"

That's a profound father-wound.

The problem with wounds is that unless they're healed, they fester. Sometimes you can see the damage immediately, but often the results of that wound don't surface until later in life. It's like a broken bone that wasn't set properly. It is never as strong as it once was, and you don't realize it until you need to rely upon the strength that you used to have. But it's just not there.

Now let's fast-forward to David as a father.

There were many things David excelled at during his life. But as far as I can tell, being a father wasn't one of them. In fact, at the end of David's life, one of his sons, Adonijah, sets out to overtake his throne. We read a striking statement about David's lack of parenting abilities: "[Adonijah's] father had never inter-

fered with him by asking, 'Why do you behave as you do?'"
(1 Kings 1:6).

Did you catch that line? David never asked his son, "Why
do you behave as you do?" In other words, David was a detached,
indifferent, aloof father.

As a boy, Adonijah may have pulled his sister's hair, or spat
on one of his younger brothers, or said curse words at the dinner
table.

David never said a thing.

As a teenager, Adonijah may have hung around with the
wrong crowd. He may have scorned his teachers, or had girlfriends of ill repute, or mocked God.

David never said a thing.

That kind of poor parenting is bound to catch up with any
father!

We begin to see some of the dysfunctions in David's family
back in 2 Samuel 13. Another son, Amnon, fell head over heels
in love with his half sister, Tamar. Amnon desperately wanted to
get his hands on her, but she was unavailable—for a lot of reasons! So Amnon decided to take matters into his own hands and
raped his own half sister.

A few chapters later, King David heard the whole story and
was enraged. But, again, we read nothing about him disciplining
his son.

David never said a thing.

Same pattern.

I don't know about you, but if I were the father of this
family, I would have a very good reason to discipline my son!

What was going on inside the mind of David? How did he refuse to get involved in such a horrible situation that affected two of his own children?

David's parenting reminds me of the story I heard recently about a herd of elephants in Africa. Because of a regional drought, all of the older male bull elephants in this particular herd had died. Young male elephants ran everything. It didn't take long before these young elephants were totally out of control. They started ripping up trees, destroying villages, and killing people. Nobody knew what to do.

Some zoologists were called in to study the elephants. They determined that there was only one thing to be done. They found some older bull elephants from another herd and transported them into this group via helicopters.

The zoologists reported that the older elephants stood around a few minutes to assess the situation. They saw how out of control the younger bull elephants were. Then they acted swiftly, immediately pinning the younger elephants to the ground with their heads. Try as they might, the younger elephants couldn't get up because the older elephants held them to the ground. This went on for hours. The older elephants were showing the younger elephants who the bosses were.

In a sense, the older elephants were fathering the younger ones.

I don't mean to say you need to hold your child's head to the ground with an elephant tusk. I mean when there's a lack of fathering, things inevitably go astray. Young elephants get out of control. Children get out of control. When there are no fathers around, it's like trying to get kids to a destination without a map. There's no sense of direction for the young. You don't know which way to go. There's not an example you can look to in order to know if you're heading the right way.

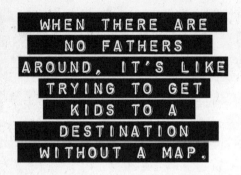

WHEN THERE ARE NO FATHERS AROUND, IT'S LIKE TRYING TO GET KIDS TO A DESTINATION WITHOUT A MAP.

If in David's family the issues stopped there, that would be one thing. But they didn't. Absalom was so enraged by his brother Amnon's actions and by his father's passiveness that he took matters into his own hands. He let his anger simmer with one thing on his mind: revenge. Two years after Amnon's terrible atrocity, Absalom committed one of his own. He had Amnon killed while at a sheep-shearing party. Absalom murdered his own brother.

Things just kept getting worse and worse. In 2 Samuel 15–17, Absalom's father-wound really started to take its toll. First, he secretly won over the hearts of the people in Israel so that he could become king, dethroning his father in the process. He then declared himself king and waged war against his father, David. He even went to his father's palace and slept with David's concubines in front of all Israel. Absalom did this to humiliate his father and to reject any authority that his father ever might have had over him.

A few verses later we read that these actions cost Absalom his own life.

At this point, David finally said something. He lamented. He grieved all the wrong that had happened.

WHAT DAVID DID RIGHT

David failed as a father in so many ways. But Scripture gives us one example of where he did the right thing, even in the midst of making mistakes.

Whenever tragedy strikes us, from a father-wound or otherwise, we all have a choice to make. We either become angry, bitter, and turn our backs on God—or we turn to God, knowing that He is the only one we can trust, we can hope in, and who can make things right.

In many senses, David's life is an amazing example of what it means to humble ourselves and put our lives in the hands of God—even when there's been tragedy. Even when the things that have been so precious to us have been taken away. Even when there seems to be no hope.

A few chapters before Absalom's death, Scripture indicates that David learned one of the greatest lessons in his life.

When David committed adultery with Bathsheba and purposely had her husband killed in battle, this was arguably the lowest point of his life. David could have justified his sin—he was never parented correctly; he was just acting out his father-wound. He could have turned away from God and perhaps become one of the wickedest kings who ever lived.

But this wasn't in David's heart. He sinned, as we all do, but

David was bigger than his sin. He humbled himself and chose a relationship with God. He tells God, "Against you, you only, I have sinned" (Ps. 51:4). David got it. It was his fear of God and his desire for relationship with God that caused him to repent.

The consequences of David's sin still cost him. In this case, it was the life of his newborn son. David did all he could do to save the life of his baby. He fasted. He prayed. He wouldn't get off the floor. In fact, his servants were concerned that David himself would die.

Let's put ourselves in David's shoes for a moment. Think about a time in life when you've begged God for something, or maybe you begged God that something wouldn't happen, but it turned out the opposite of what you thought. How did you survive?

David survived by worshipping. He turned to the Lord, not away from Him. The very moment David's servants told him that his son had died, David did something that was, quite frankly, amazing. He immediately got up off the floor, washed, put on new clothes, and went into the sanctuary to worship.

This is an example of grace.

No matter what sort of father-wound we have, God is always there.

No matter what sort of pain that wound is causing in our lives today, God is always there.

No matter what sort of damage we might have inflicted on our children, God is always there.

The answer is always our turning to God. In God we find

acceptance, an answer to our repentance, a security for our fears, a leader to follow, a heavenly Father we can trust.

David's faith was in something that this world could not offer. It didn't matter how bad the circum- stances were. He didn't care how impossible things seemed. The most important thing on this earth to David was to worship the Lord.

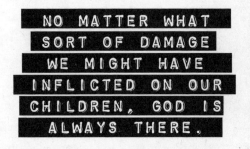

NO MATTER WHAT SORT OF DAMAGE WE MIGHT HAVE INFLICTED ON OUR CHILDREN, GOD IS ALWAYS THERE.

We might struggle with a kind of sin that is so dark, so bad, so evil, we can barely look at ourselves in the mirror every morning. Or it may just be little sins that we commit here and there. It really doesn't matter.

When we are sinned against, we often find ourselves sinning. That is true in the lives of both Brant and King David. But Christ can break that cycle. Christ longs to be the Father God many of us have never had—and all of us long for.

Here is our invitation: God intimately knew us before we lived in the sin, and He intimately knows us now, while we're walking in the midst of our sin. He has paid the price for the sin. And He welcomes us home with open arms.

Just like David did, will we turn to the Lord today?

David had great successes, and he had great failures. But the one thing David knew beyond a shadow of a doubt was that if the Lord wasn't with him, David had nothing. Anything David could accomplish on his own would pass away. The only way he would find true meaning, true significance, and true happiness was to follow after the ways of the Lord. That was more important to him than life itself.

OUR GOOD FATHER, GOD

I don't mean for this chapter to be a guidebook on parenting skills. I mean it to be an honest examination of our lives before the Lord.

When we look back at the fathering we received, what do we find? Was our dad someone who built strengths into our lives, or did his imperfections cause a wound in our hearts? Chances are, it was a bit of both.

How do we deal with those wounds today? Do we run from them, or mask them in some sort of illicit practice, or let them dictate the kind of parent we are today?

Or do we talk about those wounds with the trusted men in our lives? Do we uncover our secrets and rob them of their power? Do we look to the Lord and find new examples of what it means to be a true Father?

In my own life, I've had to relearn what it means to be a father. And there is hope for all of us who find ourselves with poor examples of what it means to be a father. I wanted to know what it meant to be a good father, so I had to truly encounter who God is. I still encounter Him and His character—and God knows I haven't nearly arrived. God continually gives me the grace to be the man I need to be.

How do you encounter God? It's simple. Begin with

Scripture. Read it. Ingest it. Take it into your life and heart. God reveals Himself through the pages of the Bible.

In Psalm 68:5-6, God is called "a father to the fatherless, a defender of widows," someone who "sets the lonely in families." This is the type of good Father we have.

I think of God's relationship with Adam in the Garden of Eden. God walked with Adam in the cool of the day. God established the foundations of relationship there.

> THERE IS HOPE FOR ALL OF US WHO FIND OURSELVES WITH POOR EXAMPLES OF WHAT IT MEANS TO BE A FATHER.

I think of the type of relationship Jesus had with God the Father. God led and guided Jesus, and God was a source of goodness, strength, and truth.

Jeremiah 29:11–13 says that God has good plans for us, plans to give us a hope and a future. God is not trying to harm us. As a good Father, He always has our best interest in mind. Our heavenly Father wants what's best for us.

John 14 talks about how God will never leave us as orphans. God will never abandon us. This is the type of good Father we have.

Do you want to know this type of Father in your life?

Grace is available. God is the good Father who always scans the horizon for us, waiting to call us home.

REFLECTIONS FOR THOSE WHO CARE
5

TAMMY MALTBY

A friend told me recently about an article that highlighted the one hundred most fascinating and successful women of the year. They were surgeons, lawyers, politicians, scientists, business CEOs, professors, fighter pilots—women who were highly disciplined, educated, and successful.

One of the questions asked of these women was, "Tell us about the relationship and role your father had in your life." Without exception, every woman said her father played a very important role. But exactly what kind of role was the real, compelling question. For the interview, each woman could choose between describing her father in three ways:

- Dad was dominant, militant, demanding, and expecting of much.
- Dad was outwardly nurturing, affectionately expressive, and always emotionally connecting.
- Dad was passive, uninvolved, absent, gone, or lacking emotional connection.

The results were divided almost evenly between numbers one and two. But there were no women who reported a number-three dad. *None.*

Let that sink in.

The point is that no matter what type of father you are, your personality will drive some of how you relate to your children. You may be stern or you may be affectionate. But what is most important is that you are there. Press into your role as a father. Don't pull back; be willing to begin again if you have had a rough start; keep pressing into the hearts of your children. No father is perfect—none. Only our heavenly Father is perfect. He will never forget us, leave us, or abandon us. God knows our heartbeat and our every pain. He is all about new beginnings.

Remember:

It is never too late to change.

It is never too late to begin.

It is never too late to ask for forgiveness and give it freely.

It is never too late unless you choose to walk away.

KEY SCRIPTURE

A father to the fatherless . . . is God in his holy dwelling. God sets the lonely in families. (Ps. 68:5–6)

WORD OF GRACE

"No matter who your father is or was, whether a great man or someone who left a lot to be desired, there is something in him that you can learn from, something that will make you a better person." —Al Roker

CHAPTER 6

"I LOVE BOOZE"
The Destructive Trap of Substance Abuse

Real men drink booze—at least, that's the way advertisers portray it.

Booze is thickly marketed to us during every Super Bowl. It fuels our car races and poker tournaments. It's billed as the quintessential social lubricant to every barbecue and office party.

Turn on the TV or watch almost any movie, and booze thunders at us from the backs of Clydesdale-pulled wagons. Booze is handed to us by our bikini-clad girlfriend when we're at the beach. Booze is a father's golden-wrapped gift to his adult son at Christmas. And booze is our ever-present manly reward for a job well done.

If we believe all that's shown to us, we guys love booze.

It would seem that a lot of us partake of the stuff. According to a recent survey, more than half of all American men regularly drink alcohol. About one-fifth of us have had one or more episodes of binge drinking within the past month. And about one in sixteen guys classifies himself as a "heavy" drinker.[1]

Even as a Christian community, we appear to be switching positions on this issue.

Fifty years ago, lines were drawn more rigidly. Drinking, card playing, gambling, dancing, moviegoing—they were all outlawed. Today, some churches continue to teach total abstinence from alcohol. Although I don't agree that the Bible teaches that, I respect that position.

Personally, I believe that Scripture allows drinking in moderation. Like so many things such as eating or working or exercising or sexuality—drinking can be part of a grace-filled life if practiced in moderation. Many Christian guys I know enjoy a glass of wine with dinner or a cold beer on a summer afternoon.

I'm certainly not enthusiastically promoting the use of booze. Just watch a couple episodes of *Cops,* and it's easy to see that alcohol used in excess impairs judgment, inflames passions, and invites violence. It is the common link in car accidents, child abuse, divorce, fighting, theft, rape, and all-around stupidity. Ephesians 5:18 explicitly condemns drunkenness with good reason.

Alcohol is part of our culture whether we like it or not, and it's not a simple issue. Yet—and here's where the issue gets more complex for good Christian guys—I don't really believe that booze is the problem. Booze *exposes* the problem, so I picked booze as the catalyst for this chapter because it's presented as so much a part of male culture. The issue could just as well be sexuality or workaholism, or any of the other addictions that plague men's lives. In all, the root question is the same: what needs are we trying to meet by looking to something external to fill those needs?

You see, it's too convenient to look at something external

and blame that, without looking at the internal. In other words, if John has his lips locked on the bottle, then all we should do is just get rid of the bottle, right?

But John's real problem is not external; it's something internal. By drinking, John is trying to fulfill an inner need. The drinking is only a Band-Aid to cover his hurt, his loneliness, his anger, his frustration, or whatever.

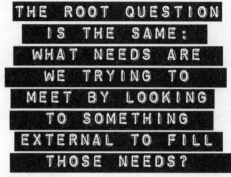

THE ROOT QUESTION IS THE SAME: WHAT NEEDS ARE WE TRYING TO MEET BY LOOKING TO SOMETHING EXTERNAL TO FILL THOSE NEEDS?

If we simply take the bottle away, John will find another external "solution" in an attempt to fill that need.

Every human is susceptible to this pattern. We make a choice to partake of a substance that gives us a feeling we like, at least at first. Then at some point we become dependent on that substance to get us through the day or night. Soon we need more and more to get the desired effect. Then we're trapped. We find ourselves unable to get ourselves unattached, no matter how hard we try. That's a good, basic description of an addiction.

The road from casual partaker to addict is always a slippery slope. Have you ever heard that voice in your own head or in the words of someone you care about? It's the one that whispers, "Just one more"—though it's almost never just one.

Or "Just a little won't hurt"—though it's not really a little, and it usually does hurt somebody.

Or, famously, "I can stop this anytime I want"—when it's just not true.

The voice that keeps telling us, against all reason, that we really *need* to go where we don't want to go . . . and that other people might get trapped, but we won't.

That's the voice that, under the right conditions, any one of us can start listening to. It's the lying, persistent, deadly voice of addiction.

What do we do if we're caught in its grip?

DON'S STORY

Don had a classic Southern Baptist upbringing. His family did all the right Christian things. External righteousness was the norm, and Don responded to the expectations at first. But he grew up trying to please so many people he ended up with an ulcer at age fifteen. Everyone had such high hopes for him. Don could sing and write music; even as a teenager, he was a gifted worship leader and could lead people into the presence of the Lord. He surely couldn't disappoint.

His parents never drank, but one Christmas his dad received a gift of Seagrams 7 and hid the bottle in the back of the pantry. Don remembers the night they left for a church outing and he took it upon himself to pull it down. Alcohol had always been presented to him as something evil. Portrayals crossed the line of exaggeration—if you drank booze, you'd turn into some kind of seven-headed monster. Don decided to test the waters. He poured himself a glass, cut it with some 7-Up, and drank. Suddenly Don didn't feel as anxious or uptight anymore. *Wait a minute,* he thought, *this is some pretty good stuff!* His conclusion: people had been lying to him about alcohol. *Figures!*

Don married early in life and began working for his dad. Stresses hit immediately. His dad was always on his case about something, and it made Don feel like a kid again. Then his new wife got pregnant. How would Don pay the bills? What would he do to deal with the stress?

He started drinking a little bit. It took the edge off at night—just a little wine, beer, maybe a couple of margaritas. It wasn't a big deal, of course. What was a big deal was *why* he was drinking. The trap started for Don right there. He was drinking to meet a need inside—he needed the stress to go away. Forget about creating a plan to obtain additional money to help with a new baby. *Nah, that's not necessary. A drink will do.* And that's where he went wrong.

Things became harder. His new wife, whom he was madly in love with, started to exhibit strange symptoms in her body—numbness, fatigue, tingling, losing her balance from time to time. A neurologist diagnosed her with multiple sclerosis. Now what would they do?

Don took a position as worship pastor at a local church so he could stay home and care for his wife. Politics and stress set in, and Don continued with his secret habit of coping. His wife's MS began to advance. More episodes and flare-ups occurred. Eventually, she needed to use a walker around the house and a wheelchair whenever they went out. Don's drinking became heavier and heavier. He started lying to his wife when she noticed the amount he drank.

"Honey, have you had more than one glass of wine?" she would ask.

"Only one glass," Don would say. After all, it was only *one glass*—he had just filled it a dozen times.

Soon, he started forgetting things. Who did he just talk to on the phone? What did he say? Sometimes he woke up with bruises, not knowing where they came from. Furniture would be turned over and broken, and Don would have no idea how things got that way.

Don became a pro at hiding his drinking, even doing research to develop an effective system for hiding his habit. He would go to five different liquor stores and buy booze so nobody would suspect anything. He would only drink rum and tequila because it wouldn't make him sick or hungover.

But his nerves became increasingly jittery. A drink was the only thing that would calm him down. He couldn't wait to get off the stage leading worship each Sunday morning so he could settle down with his bottle.

That was his life for five years: drinking every night through the week, getting up each Sunday to lead worship, going home and drinking more because clarity was starting to set in.

Don tried to stop a hundred times. He would tell himself, "I'll only drink when we go out to a restaurant." Or "I'll only drink beer." Or "I'll only drink at someone's house." But none of his plans worked.

And people were starting to catch on. It's hard to keep a life like that secret forever. But he had to uphold a good Christian veneer. Don was a pastor, for heaven's sake. Pastors don't wrestle with addictions!

Once, Don was out of town and drank obsessively. The next morning he woke up, felt terrible, and threw away all his liquor bottles. Later that night, he found himself rummaging through the trash bin outside the hotel to recover those precious bottles. That was the rock bottom he needed.

He started to meet with a group of trusted friends at a men's ministry called the Samson Society, run by author and speaker Nate Larkin. Seeing how these guys were open about their sins and struggles gave Don the courage to go out on a limb. One night he said casually, "Hey guys, I think I might have a drinking problem."

That was Don's start back to the truth.

Nate befriended Don and helped him start to admit what was really going on. Nate invited him to an AA meeting. Another friend asked Don some hard questions.

"Don, do you think you're an alcoholic?"

"No, no, are you kidding? I'm a Christian who drinks every now and then. Not an alcoholic!"

"Really?"

"Well . . . I'm not quite sure."

Don finally admitted that his problem was bigger than he was. The key for him was surrendering—really surrendering—his life to the Lord. When Don started talking about what was truly happening in his life, he could finally admit to his friends what was going on. Because he was honest, they felt the freedom to be honest in return. It created a whole new set of trusting relationships that weren't based on veneers anymore. Some of his friends confessed to similar struggles.

That honesty has been the catalyst for real change. Don says today, "I never thought I would have this many friends—good, deep relationships—and I can talk to them about anything. I'm finding that now I'm seeing the world through different eyes. I'm not as concerned about what people think or performing for people. I'm able to confront things in my life that are bothering me."

I wish I could say everything changed instantly for the better in Don's world. But things became harder before they got better. The difference was how Don handled the stress.

He got healthier, but his wife didn't. During one eight-month stretch, she was in the hospital for five of those months. Many of Don's days were spent arguing with insurance companies.

Just recently, he and his wife were home in bed. It was late, and she got up for a glass of water. All of a sudden, Don heard something strange in the other room. He went in to find his wife facedown on the floor. She had fallen and shattered her arm. He immediately rushed her to the hospital. What he can't imagine is if he had been drunk that night. She fell at two a.m., and that would not have been a good time for him. There is no way he would have heard her. How long would she have lain on that floor, on her face, if he had still been drinking?

IS THERE HOPE?

Overuse of booze is a tough issue. I've struggled with drinking over the years. Before I fully yielded my life to the Lord, drinking and drugs were an almost daily part of my life.

And I know firsthand that addictions can have plenty of internal causes. But almost all of these causes stem from the desire to experience pleasure and escape pain.

God made us with these desires and He made them good. He wanted us to be able to enjoy His creation (pleasure) and to avoid what isn't good for us (pain).

But as is so often true with God's gifts, we fallen people tend to misuse them. So in our drive to find pleasure and escape pain, we turn to objects that are inadequate, dangerous, or both. Instead of rejoicing and finding pleasure in God's goodness and the beauty of creation, we enjoy the buzz of a couple of beers. Or instead of coming to God with our pain or leaving the source of pain behind us, we seek to numb the feelings with a couple of cocktails.

If we like the unhealthy experience, we do it again . . . and again . . . until it takes on a life of its own. A habit is born. We become physically, emotionally, and spiritually attached to whatever we're taking or doing. If the

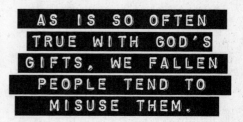

AS IS SO OFTEN TRUE WITH GOD'S GIFTS, WE FALLEN PEOPLE TEND TO MISUSE THEM.

process is allowed to continue, we reach the point where we simply can't stop on our own. We become addicted.

Unquestionably, addiction is sin. It's a misuse of God's gifts, a missing of the mark, as Romans 3:23 describes. It's also a form of idolatry, in that something or someone other than God—in this case, booze—becomes the essential center of our universe. No matter what we profess with our lips or think with our mind, if we're addicted we are essentially worshiping the object of our addiction.

And addiction is intertwined with sin in so many other ways. It involves behavior that hurts ourselves and others and gets in the way of our relationship with God—lies and deception, drunkenness, sexual immorality, abuse, even murder. And one person's sin can push another person toward addiction. Thus an alcoholic father's abuse influences a child to numb the pain by taking drugs.

Addiction is a sin problem—there's no way around it. But simply addressing the sin element in addiction tends to be ineffective because addiction is also a sickness, a complicated disease that affects the whole person—body, mind, emotions, and spirit.

Alcohol and drug dependency are actually listed as diseases by the American Medical Association. In fact, almost all addictions fit the basic description of a chronic disease. There is some evidence that susceptibility to certain addictions is genetic. There is a clear and predictable progression of symptoms. The attachment is chronic; it doesn't go away on its own. It's also progressive; it gets worse without treatment. It's treatable, though relapses are not uncommon. And if not treated, addictions can lead to added complications and even death.

Some Christians object to describing addiction as disease because they believe it excuses an addict of responsibility. "If you say you're sick," they charge, "that means you just couldn't help it—it's an excuse to sin." But I have absolutely no problem with thinking of addiction as both a sin and a sickness. In fact, I think recovery is more likely if we think that way.

After all, there are plenty of purely physical illnesses that are at least partially caused or spread by human sin and irresponsibility—lung cancer from smoking, heart attacks from overeating, STDs from illicit sex, colds spread by not covering the mouth or washing hands. Treatment of any disease calls for responsibility on the part of the victim—taking medications, eating right, exercising, physical or mental therapy, whatever the doctor orders.

And God *always* requires our cooperation in the process of our own healing. He asks us to repent and accept forgiveness and forgive others. He requires us to adjust our lifestyles and cooperate with doctors to be healed of physical illness. He wants us to look at ourselves honestly and kindly—to examine our hearts and understand our emotions and forgive ourselves to be healed of emotional diseases. And when we find ourselves trapped in addictions, all of the above apply.

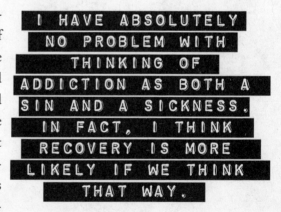

I HAVE ABSOLUTELY NO PROBLEM WITH THINKING OF ADDICTION AS BOTH A SIN AND A SICKNESS. IN FACT, I THINK RECOVERY IS MORE LIKELY IF WE THINK THAT WAY.

Thinking of addiction as both sin and disease doesn't excuse us from responsibility. In fact, it asks a lot of us. It asks us to be involved in the process of healing.

And if we think we aren't susceptible to an addiction, we've got another think coming.

We've all experienced a momentary lapse in good decision making. You know what I mean—it's like all of a sudden all of our good judgment flies out the window. We look back and we're not even sure how it happened. But it does happen, even to the best of us.

That's exactly what happened to a good Christian guy named Noah, whose story is told in the book of Genesis. On the outside it looked like he knew everything there was to know about sin—he saw God deal with it firsthand. But even that didn't stop Noah from making one mistake. And that one mistake had ramifications that lasted for generations.

> IF WE THINK WE AREN'T SUSCEPTIBLE TO AN ADDICTION WE'VE GOT ANOTHER THINK COMING.

WHAT WAS NOAH THINKING?!

As a father of six kids, whenever I hear about the story of Noah, my mind immediately snaps to the dozens of plastic animals scattered all over my house.

Although Noah is a great children's story, there is a deeper issue behind Noah's life. He was a profoundly deep man of faith who had a few darker issues that he didn't deal with. In moments of weakness these dark issues came back to bite him.

The story of Noah is familiar to most of us: Noah was surrounded by a community of people who had absolutely no care about God or His ways. Scripture describes the level of atrociousness this way: "Every inclination of the thoughts of [humanity's] heart was only evil all the time" (Gen. 6:5).

So God, in His righteousness, chose to wipe the slate clean. He sent a huge flood to destroy humanity. Noah built an ark and was saved along with his family and two of every kind of animal. After time, the water dried up, Noah and his family came out of the ark, and God put a rainbow in the sky as a covenant that He would never again destroy humanity by a flood.

When this story is told in Sunday school, the story usually ends there: a happy ending. But there's one critical part to Noah's life that comes after that—and this one's not so happy.

Scripture describes Noah as "a man of the soil" (Gen. 9:20). One of the first things Noah did after climbing out of the ark was to plant a vineyard, make some wine, and get drunk. The lesson is obvious: even a very good man, when drunk, can forget all he knows to be true and do foolish things, and Noah was no exception. While drunk, Noah took off his clothes and "lay uncovered inside his tent" (v. 21).

One of Noah's sons, Ham, came into the tent and saw his father's nakedness. Apparently, Ham thought this was quite comical and invited all of his brothers to have a look at the show. His brothers did the honorable thing and refused to shame their father. Instead, they brought a blanket and covered their father's nakedness.

Noah woke up from his drunken stupor and found out what had happened. Instead of dealing directly with his son, Ham, he directed a curse at his grandson, Ham's son, Canaan. In other words, Noah was so angry and shamed that he cursed future generations.

It's a crazy story, to be sure. Noah had been reminded many times of God's dealing with sin: God hates sin so much He destroyed the whole world because of it. Yet Noah's actions defied logic. Noah ran to the very sin he knew God hates. And the repercussions last for generations to come.

Much of the time our sins are never just our sins. Sure they affect us in numerous ways, but they also affect those who are closest to us, and they have implications on our families—sometimes for generations. This thought that my sins could affect my children is too terrible for me to bear. It puts the holy fear of God in me. The last thing on this earth I want to do is repeat the sins of my father, and of myself, on the next generation.

Have you ever really thought about that? The sins you are committing now could manifest themselves in your children's children. Wow! It's one thing for me to think that my sins might be destroying my life; it's a totally different thing for me to see that my sins could have a terrible effect on the lives of my children and my grandchildren. In theological terms, this is called generational sin.

I am certainly a product of this kind of sin. The father-wound handed to me by my absentee father affected me in many negative areas throughout my life. There are still times as an adult when I suffer personally and relationally from not having a loving birth family.

But I don't want you to think for a second that I'm a victim. The other side of the coin here is when we blame our past or our parents for everything wrong in our lives today. Although it may be true that generational sin has an impact on us, we men must take full responsibility for where we are today. You and I cannot change the past, but we can certainly change the future. If I walk around with my tail between my legs because of what happened to me in previous years, I end up giving away all my power to things I can't control.

Noah didn't take responsibility for his sin, and his family paid the price generation after generation. Shem and Japheth were blessed by their father and went on to accomplish great things. But Ham's son was cursed.

May nothing like this ever happen in our lives.

HELP WHEN YOU'RE STUCK

So what do we do?

What do we do when we run to an outward substance instead of dealing with our inner issues?

What do we do if we find ourselves caught in an addiction to alcohol—or any addiction, for that matter?

The sin-disease of addiction may be one of the trickiest afflictions we humans encounter in this fallen world. Involved in it are issues of heredity and environment, brain chemistry and spiritual connection, what we can do and what we can't do, release and relapse.

Every day, it seems, someone discovers something new about how addiction works and offers a new idea about how it can be treated. But even with treatment and improvement, many experts believe addictions are never fully cured.

Neither is the problem of sin, for that matter. Just as all good Christian guys remain sinners, experts tell us that addicts remain addicts all their lives—their brains are permanently altered to respond to the addictive substance or behavior.

That doesn't sound very hopeful. But the good news is that experts also say that any addict can live free as long as he is able to stay away from the addictive substance or behavior, even though he is always a few steps away from falling into the trap once more.

THE SIN-DISEASE OF ADDICTION MAY BE ONE OF THE TRICKIEST AFFLICTIONS WE HUMANS ENCOUNTER IN THIS FALLEN WORLD.

So the subject is complicated as well as heartbreaking. And I'm certainly not in a position to unravel it all for you. Even if I had all the answers, I wouldn't try to squeeze them into a simplistic, zipped-up version that fits into a single chapter of a book.

More to the point, there are already plenty of in-depth programs out there to help people recover from addictions—excellent counseling centers and organizations, superb rehab setups, and community-based groups such as the time-tested, spiritually based, and highly practical programs based on the twelve steps of Alcoholics Anonymous. There are good articles to give you information, support groups to encourage you, wise and savvy pastors and Christian counselors to help you as you struggle to recover or find help for a loved one.

So I have no intentions of using this chapter to fully outline the healing process. But I do have a suggestion about where it has to start.

If we never choose to dabble in booze or cigarettes or porn or toxic religion, we can save ourselves a lot of grief.

THE PLACE WE NEED TO START IS A SIMPLE ONE. IT'S SURRENDERING TO THE LORD.

But if we're there—once we're addicted or involved with an addict—there is one place that we *need* to go.

It's toward the truth about our sin and brokenness. It's toward the reality that we are no longer in control of our lives. And it's toward the Truth that really can set us free.

I am a firm believer that the first step we need to take is not to try to clean up our lives on our own. We don't need to go get our life "right," whatever that means, before we're in a position to be free.

The place we need to start is a simple one.

It's surrendering to the Lord.

Our invitation is to come to the place where we can freely and honestly receive the resources God is surrounding us with right now—namely, His grace and forgiveness. God knows our addictions, He knows our sins, and He loves us just the same. The act of surrendering all we are to Him is an act that brings freedom. We don't have to work at it. But we must accept His grace, receive it, and allow it to take over our life. The easy part is knowing that God's grace is available; the hard part is trading all we have become for all that He is.

The first step also involves taking 100 percent responsibility for ourselves.

This is how we begin to walk on the path toward freedom. A key characteristic of any addict's life is to blame others for his issues. Typically he can't think about all the negative behavioral patterns that are present in who he's become without putting the responsibility on someone or something else. To admit he's actually an addict means an admission of failure, and the thought of being a failure is too much to bear.

The truth is that all of us have failed in many ways, but we are never failures. Remember, taking 100 percent responsibility gives you your power back. You allowed yourself to get used to this situation, but you can find your way out.

The good news is this: despite Noah's failures, he's still listed as an incredible man of faith. As far as I know, his sin of loving booze too much is the only one of his sins ever mentioned in the Bible. I'm sure it's there for good reason—for us to learn from and to realize that there are consequences for our sins, and that God has a better plan for us than that. In the end, Noah goes down in history as a great man, not perfect, but great. He is mentioned in Hebrews 11 as one of the heroes of the faith.

Welcome to grace—for Noah, for us.

That's one of the things I love so much about the Bible. It isn't just filled with stories of people who've done everything perfectly. It's filled with stories of flawed men and women who somehow recognized they were flawed but overcame that and put all of their hope and trust in God. When they did this, God always made something great out of their lives.

God always extended grace, mercy, and compassion when they turned to Him.

And God will do the same for us.

REFLECTIONS FOR THOSE WHO CARE
6

TAMMY MALTBY

There is an old saying that goes, "Sin will take you further than you ever want to go, keep you longer than you ever want to stay, and cost you more than you ever want to pay."

I am confident the writer of this quote was referring to addiction—anything that falsely anesthetizes our pain and keeps us from dealing with the truth. Remember, Jesus not only wants us to deal honestly with our pain, but He provides the light for a new way of living.

When a friend is trapped by a substance, it can feel overwhelming for those who love him. This problem can be destructive in his life and in the lives of those he loves. Yet no problem is too large for the Lord to handle. Meditating on that simple truth can help see us through our darkest days.

Substance abuse issues typically require a team of people helping a person. It also requires the willingness of the addict. You may need to enlist the help of others to help your friend. You may also need to be patient and wait for your friend to reach rock bottom. It is impossible to help someone who doesn't believe he needs help.

Ultimately, God knows all of our addictions and sins, and He loves us just the same. The act of surrendering all we are to Him brings freedom. We don't have to work at it. But we must accept His grace, receive it, and allow it to take over our life. As Tom said, "The easy part is knowing God's grace is available; the hard part is trading all we have become for all that He is."

KEY SCRIPTURE

Above all, love one another deeply, because love covers a multitude of sins. (1 Pet. 4:8)

WORD OF GRACE

"The more I reminded myself of God's sovereign power, the less intimidated I was by the things I couldn't control." — Pam Vredevelt

CHAPTER 7

"I DON'T LIKE TO FEEL"
The Difficulty of Being a Three-Dimensional Man

Now there's a question men hate to answer. Someone—often a wife or girlfriend—asks us how we *feel*, and our tendency is to glance at our watch, or wish we were playing video games with our son, or become defensive and demand to know why that person has asked such a stupid question in the first place.

When someone asks us how we *feel*, we're forced to think up a name for an emotion. And naming emotions isn't typically something we're used to doing. Men are seldom taught what an emotion is, what it looks like, or even what it's called.

Think I'm kidding here? Take a short self-inventory. Quick—list the first five emotions you can think of.

Emotions, huh? Well, let's see . . . there's . . . uh . . . anger . . . (one)

. . . .and . . . .uh . . . uh . . . rage . . . (two)

. . . and . . . uh . . . hunger? Isn't that an emotion? Okay, that's three . . .

So we've got anger, rage, hunger, and . . . uh . . .

I posed this same question to a group of women recently, and do you know how many emotions they listed?

More than one hundred and thirty.

I had no idea that *giggly* was an emotion. I don't think I've ever felt *giggly* before, but according to this group of women, sure enough, you could feel *giggly* if you chose to.

You could also feel rejected, cranky, pensive, optimistic, hyper, guilty, lonely, restless, mellow, annoyed, numb, productive, stressed, devious, thankful, bouncy, sleepy, happy, sad, depressed, pessimistic, surprised, jealous, jubilant, chipper, determined, frustrated, contemplative, morose, indifferent . . . and about one hundred more!

Who knew? We men are more into burly stuff, not naming emotions. Men like to lift weights and race cars and eat steak and go four-wheeling. Our idea of a good time is to hike into the wilderness and shoot large animals and gut the carcasses and have them stuffed and displayed over our mantelpieces for all our other guy friends to see and admire. Ask me how I *feel* about all that, and I'd say it feels *pretty dang cool.* (Now there's an emotion I don't think was on the women's list.)

But ask me how I feel about stuff on a day-to-day basis, and I tend to clam up. Right or wrong, men often believe that being in touch with your emotions is dangerously close to "being in touch with your feminine side." And who wants that?

Here's where the subject of emotions becomes tricky.

We men have emotions whether we can name them or not.

And our emotions can come out at the strangest places and times.

And when those emotions do come out, often we're not sure what to do with them. Usually we think we

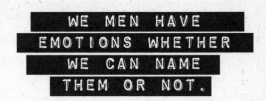

WE MEN HAVE EMOTIONS WHETHER WE CAN NAME THEM OR NOT.

need to control them, or shut them off, or stuff them deep inside us where no one can ever find them. Emotions can be difficult to get a handle on, especially when we admit that fundamental confession that men are supposed to say: "I don't like to *feel.*"

Don't like to *feel,* eh? Has anything like this ever happened to you?

- At dinner one night, you asked your daughter to eat something on her plate, but your wife said she didn't have to. That one little thing set you off and you exploded. It had been a hard day at work and that was the last straw. You slammed your fist down on the table, snapped at your daughter, and cursed at your wife. Emotions? Whatever. You don't like to *feel.*

- Or you did just the opposite. Same situation, but you shut down instead. You left the table and sat in front of the TV. You just couldn't handle one more divisive thing right then, so you masked how you felt by pretending the situation didn't exist. Emotions? No way, man. It's a whole lot easier to pretend you don't *feel* anything.

- Or something overwhelming came up—maybe it's a family member in the hospital. You planned your escape. You buried yourself in books to research the medical condition, or you headed down to the bar, or you worked extra hours to avoid the hospital. Whatever your pattern was, you dealt with stress by running from it. *Feel* something? No thanks. Feelings hurt too much.

- A colleague of yours received a big promotion and a fat raise. You shook his hand and slapped his back with all the other well-wishers, but deep down you wanted to slug him at the same time. Part of our emotional makeup? No way. Jealousy is something we could never admit to *feeling*. We don't like to *feel*.

- You wonder why all those people at church are just so smiley. They're always talking about how great God is and singing songs about falling down at His feet and stuff. You're a believer, but you've never really *felt* anything in your relationship with Christ before. Certainly not like that, anyway.

Who wants to *feel* something when emotions can be such hard stuff? It's far easier to pretend we're emotionless creatures.

WE HAVE FEELINGS WHETHER WE ADMIT IT OR NOT.

But this is fact: as men we were created as human beings who have emotions. We have feelings whether we admit it or not. God has emotions. In the Bible, we see that God experiences everything from sorrow to anger to joy to holy jealousy to righteous pride.

Emotions are not wrong. Emotions are an integral part of our lives. Think of them as a backpack we carry around filled with a mix of memories, life experiences, previous reactions we've had to situations, and beliefs about our world. All of these things make us into the men we are today.

So what do we do with our emotions? How do we truly reflect our God-given characteristic of being created with feelings? How do we become more than two-dimensional men, men who only *think* and *act*, to realize our full responsibility and privilege of being three-dimensional men—men who truly know how to *think, act,* and *feel*?

When Fear Is at the Core

We men do feel things; it's just that we have a hard time identifying what we feel, then knowing what to do with that emotion.

To make matters worse, there is one emotion that tends to dominate all others in our lives. This emotion is the biggest, baddest kid on the block, and when it comes up, it tends to stifle and overshadow all other emotions.

I wish I could tell you this emotion was love, or encouragement, or maybe happiness. But it's not. Anyone have a guess as to what it is?

It's fear.

Having *fear* is not something most of us readily admit. We're macho guys—nothing makes us afraid. But I'm not talking about a fear of spiders or even a fear of public speaking (what 99 percent of us have). I'm talking about a type of fear that's deeply rooted in our psyches. This type of fear is something we seldom even realize we have. But when we lift the lid on our inner lives, the emotion of fear is at the core far more than we know. How does this type of deep, inner-core fear show up in our lives?

Dive into this a little deeper with me. Psychologist Abraham Maslow described life as a hierarchy of needs. On the bottom rungs of that hierarchy are all our primary needs, such as food, water, sex, and sleep. If any of those needs aren't met, we fight and claw and search with all our might to meet those needs. Ever seen a video of a man drowning? That's a picture of Maslow's hierarchy of needs at work. If a person can't get air, then fear and desperation set in, and the drowning man will work as hard as he can to get that need met.

At the top of Maslow's list is the need for self-actualization. Self-actualization has been defined in different ways over the years, but it's basically the need to do something significant with our lives. Self-actualization is what's being questioned whenever we look in the mirror and ask ourselves if we matter. It's our need to have purpose and meaning. If that need isn't met, the same thing will happen. Fear sets in and we'll work as hard as we can to reach that place in our life.

The rub is that it's easy to feel like we don't matter. We live in a culture that pushes us to acquire things, in order to matter. So we work harder and harder, yet we still don't have the kind of lives we're looking for. So we get stressed out, tired, and angry.

Still, that purpose and meaning eludes us. We might have a lot of stuff in the end, but little of it seems to provide any contentment, meaning, or fulfillment. Our lives become harshly cyclical. We fear that we're not doing enough, we won't have enough, or that we won't be who everybody needs us to be.

And that fear catches up with us. Has anything like this ever happened to you?

- You find yourself showing up late to meetings, missing deadlines, or not returning phone calls promptly because you are trying to please too many people and be too many places at the same time. When it comes right down to it, you are afraid of disappointing anyone.
- You become defensive when confronted with information you feel is threatening. Someone's trying to bring up a valid issue, but all you hear is, "You're a failure." You fear someone's honest critique of you, or even fear that someone else has a good opinion that's different than yours.
- Your boss asks you to do something that's borderline immoral or unethical. You feel backed against a wall but do it anyway against your better judgment. You're afraid that if you stand up to him, you'll lose your job.
- A friend asks you to attend an event that you don't want to go to, but you smile and say, "I'll try." You don't directly say no, because you're pretty sure that will hurt her feelings, and if that were to happen your friend might reject you. So you use vague, noncommittal language, and then you still don't show up.

A deep, inner fear is present in all the scenarios above. And it's present in our lives more than we think. And that can be a huge problem.

When fear becomes the primary driver in our lives, it tends to color all our other emotions and reactions. Pretty soon the highs and lows of life build up and get to us. Our fears start to rule more areas of our life than we are even aware. We find ourselves over-committed, and our emotions either pop out in unusual ways in response to what's happening around us, or we shut down emotionally because we can't handle it anymore.

Men tend to develop various ways of dealing with emotional oversaturation. Some of them we already talked about—compromising morally, substance abuse, false pride in what we have or do. Fear can emerge any number of ways.

WHEN FEAR BECOMES THE PRIMARY DRIVER IN OUR LIVES, IT TENDS TO COLOR ALL OUR OTHER EMOTIONS AND REACTIONS.

Maybe you're having a normal conversation with someone, and in a few seconds things go very wrong. The person says something that rubs you the wrong way, and your emotions come flying out! The blood rushes to your head, your face flushes, your heart starts beating fast, and you're in danger of saying and doing something you may regret. That's fear at work.

Or we get to those places where it's difficult to control other emotions: we need to express our love or admiration for somebody but find that we are just not capable, or we need to express shame or grief or stress or thankfulness or relief or anger or another emotion, but again and again we don't know what to say or do or how to act. Again, that's that type of deep, inner fear emerging in our lives.

So how do we sort out situations like that? What do we do? How do we correctly interpret situations so we can sort out the true emotion we're feeling, and then act appropriately on that emotion?

The Bible describes part of the solution this way: "Above all else, guard your heart, for it is the wellspring of life" (Prov. 4:23).

Guarding our hearts doesn't mean that we have to wall up our emotions as if they were under lock and key in a castle. But it does mean we need to watch carefully over our emotions—guard them like we'd look out for something valuable, like we'd 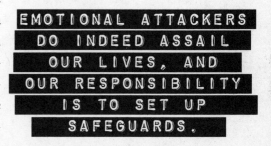 guard our families or guard our sexual purity and marital fidelity.

EMOTIONAL ATTACKERS DO INDEED ASSAIL OUR LIVES, AND OUR RESPONSIBILITY IS TO SET UP SAFEGUARDS.

This verse acknowledges that emotional attackers do indeed assail our lives, and our responsibility is to set up safeguards. We need to bring strength to the situation and surround our emotions—not to hide them away, but to let them flourish, thrive, and be healthy, as they were meant to be.

So what does this look like? Emotions occur so quickly, there's barely enough time to stop them, much less understand them, sort them out, and let them flourish.

The fuller answer involves a bit of work. Part of "guarding

our hearts" involves understanding how our emotions develop in the first place. With this uncovered, we'll be able to see the reasons we respond to certain situations as we do. Lifting the lid on our inner lives can be one of the prime steps toward living the abundant life we were meant to live.

BENEATH THE LID

In addition to my responsibilities as head of an orphanage ministry, over the years I've worked as a consultant in leadership development. I've presented seminars for leaders and managers of all sorts of businesses, including Fortune 500 companies, mid-size companies, and nonprofit organizations. This is a key component of what I teach.

In the seminars, I help men become the most capable leaders they can be. And that includes learning how to identify emotions and properly express them. For instance, we've all seen leaders fly off the handle at inappropriate times. Part of my teaching helps leaders work through those situations and know how to respond.

One of the key questions we deal with is "Where do our emotions, including the core emotion of fear, come from?"

The answer involves a bit of self-examination. Sometimes that can be painful; we're not used to lifting the lids on our inner lives. But it's a more truthful answer. Think it through with me.

The primary place emotions come from is our "life filters"—the values, beliefs, and experiences that shape how we see and interpret the world.

Every day when you get up, your life filter gets up with you. It's always switched on, and it receives information and instructs you subconsciously what to think and how to act based upon the information you receive.

For instance, if you've had a privileged upbringing where things came to you easily, you received a high degree of positive feedback over the years, and you have been loved and supported throughout life, then your life filter might be more rose-colored, meaning you're essentially an optimistic person who believes the best about people and has a high degree of hopefulness and buoyancy.

THE PRIMARY PLACE EMOTIONS COME FROM IS OUR "LIFE FILTERS"—THE VALUES, BELIEFS, AND EXPERIENCES THAT SHAPE HOW WE SEE AND INTERPRET THE WORLD.

Perhaps you've had a less privileged upbringing where people yelled at you all day long, questioned everything you said or did, and your life was marked by failure and abuse. Then your life filter might be tainted and smudged, meaning you tend to look at people with suspicion, be pessimistic in your outlook, and generally prepare for the worst to happen.

Our life filters are running twenty-four hours a day, telling us all kinds of things about our lives, relationships, and values. The filters tell us a story about people and events so fast we often don't have time to field what comes at us. We get much of our emotions—how we respond to things—based on our life filters.

Consider this: the majority of the men I interviewed for this book have one thing in common. They had some sort of traumatic event that occurred early in life that tended to color how the rest of life is viewed. That event caused a root of fear to grow. Fear began to dominate all other emotions and reactions until most of the men's behavior is now driven by fear.

Like one day when a boy was invited to sit at the lunch table with the football players. The boy was in band, and band guys and football players never mixed at that school; but for some reason, one of the players invited him to their lunch table.

The biggest football player was apparently not aware that one of his teammates had invited the band guy. He stood up and yelled at the band guy in front of everyone: "Hey faggot, what are you doing sitting at our table! We don't allow faggots to sit here. Get out before we rip your head off!"

Bam!—part of that boy's life filter was just added. Fear just found its home. Years later, that boy is now a grown man, and he's still wrestling with issues of acceptance. Personality-wise, his tendency is toward more artistic things—he still appreciates fine music, for instance. But he's careful about who he talks to about his likes and dislikes because he's afraid of the name-calling—or whatever the adult equivalent of that might be. His behavior today is rooted in the emotion of fear, which first latched hold of him because of a traumatic childhood event.

Painful events like those occur with regularity and can still be as painful to this day in the lives of grown men. Many of the men I talked to shared stories just like that one—in tears.

Some of the most impressionable events of our lives occurred when we were young children. What happened in our homes, specifically when we were under age five, had a dramatic impact on our values and beliefs as we grew up. The number one value a child has at that age is safety. It's part of God's design that young children are to be nurtured, cared for, and protected by their parents. When this doesn't happen, children are forced to find alternative means to be safe.

I identify completely with this pattern. My story is that I grew up in a broken home. As mentioned in other chapters, I didn't know my real father for sixteen years. My mother married a man who was quite abusive. My memories as a young child are ones of screaming, yelling, and physical abuse—both to my mother and to me.

In order to stay safe—both physically and emotionally— guess what I did? I retreated. I created a fantasy land in my mind and heart where everything was safe. Nothing was safe for me on the outside, so I had to create an inner world that was.

How did this affect my emotions? I shut them down. If expressing an emotion meant I might get punished for it, then I sure wasn't going to show anything. I was surrounded by chaos in my family of origin, and that taught me things about the world whether I liked it or not.

Now I'm a husband and a father. Guess what I have a hard time doing? You got it: expressing emotions healthily. My tendency has always been to withdraw emotionally. My life filter tells me that emotions are a bad thing—if you express them, you'll only get hurt.

But that doesn't work as an adult. And it's murder on a

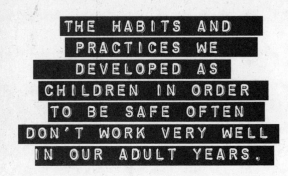

THE HABITS AND PRACTICES WE DEVELOPED AS CHILDREN IN ORDER TO BE SAFE OFTEN DON'T WORK VERY WELL IN OUR ADULT YEARS.

marriage. The habits and practices we developed as children in order to be safe often don't work very well in our adult years.

Part of the pathway to healing is to understand where these kinds of responses come from in our lives. To start paying attention. To start asking ourselves why we are afraid. It means relearning some things as an adult. Our life filters are not destined to stay the same way forever.

And we're not doomed to stay in these traps forever.

Just like Steve. He's a good Christian guy who had some emotional trauma in his past. But he's learning to lift the lid on his inner life, identify the emotion behind his behavior, and let God heal the experiences and beliefs that prompted the emotion.

STEVE'S STORY

In Steve's most honest moments, he knows he has a difficult time as an adult with his emotions. His typical emotional responses look something like this:

- If his wife upsets him in any way, he seldom deals with it directly; instead, he'll just give her a look of disgust and sulk away to the couch.

- If a friend ticks him off in any way, he ignores the friend and doesn't talk to him for weeks.
- At family gatherings, he has a hard time enjoying himself. He has a habit of saying hurtful, sarcastic things that bring an icy chill to the air.

Steve began doing some good work awhile ago in this area. He realized he didn't like how he expressed (or failed to express) his emotions. Mostly, whenever he got into any emotionally charged situation, something just shut down in his head. He didn't want to go to the truth of what he was feeling; he didn't want to interact with the emotion or identify it. Most of his emotions emerged as defense mechanisms to keep people away. He acted as though he didn't want or need anyone.

There have been many nights when Steve and his wife have been in some kind of an argument. Sometimes there's a good reason for it; other times he really can't tell what sets it off. She asks him a question about why he acts like he does, and then it starts. Steve just shuts down and goes into some kind of galactic sleep mode. Once his wife asked him a serious question, and he sat on the couch for three hours without a response. She patiently waited. Still, no response.

As Steve has tried to process his emotions in healthier moments, he's realized that he has never wanted anyone to get close to him. He's afraid of revealing anything personal about himself, even to his wife. He's always been afraid that if people had "information" on him, they would eventually use it to hurt him. The more they knew, the more opportunity they would have to stab him in the back with it. When it comes right down to it, Steve believes that people are dangerous.

Where does this come from? All of our behaviors in life come from somewhere. Why does Steve believe that people are dangerous?

Track backward and take a look at how Steve's life filter was formed.

Things started rough for Steve. When he was only three months old, his father died. As Steve grew up, he realized other kids had dads who took them to the movies, fishing, or to basketball and football games.

But Steve had no one. So he devised a fantasy world. If he had a dad, his dad would be the best dad ever! They would go everywhere together. They would wrestle and play games every night, they would go on the best hunting trips, they would be the best of friends. This was the picture Steve created in his mind. It was always a safe place for him to go.

As he grew up, a Christian summer camp became the epicenter of his life. It's what he looked forward to throughout the year. He made some good friends there of his own age, and every year he would meet awesome families with other people's dads who would take an interest in him. He loved the way that felt.

He and his mother would attend the family camps together. His mom would always make huge servings of chili and spaghetti, and the people who camped around them would always come over to eat at their tent. One little boy came over regularly for the food. Over time, he became Steve's best friend.

They hiked and climbed together, and explored the forest. Steve and the friend told each other they'd be best friends forever.

But one day the friend didn't show up. Steve walked over to the friend's tent to see if he could play. This day, the friend was acting sort of weird.

"What's the matter?" Steve asked his friend. "Why can't you come and play today?"

"My dad says I can't right now."

"Well, what about later?"

"Dad said not later, either."

"Tomorrow?"

"No."

"I don't understand," Steve said.

"Well, my dad says I can't play with you anymore because you're not a good influence on me."

Not a good influence! I imagine this is hard to hear at any age, but when you're a kid, this must just destroy you. Steve felt the rejection of his friend. He also felt it from the friend's father. Another father who abandoned him. A deep wound was created at that moment.

So what did Steve do? If friends hurt that much, he decided he wouldn't have friends. He emotionally shut down. He still has a hard time talking about it to this day.

Steve grew up knowing little about how to have or express true emotions. His mother had her own set of difficulties, and Steve seldom saw a healthy role model of dealing with emotions. So he resorted to all he knew—emotional shutdown.

Can you see how much our experiences as children affect

how we grow up as adults? These experiences when we're young form our life filters. We develop patterns and habits without even knowing. The only way to adjust our life filters is to go deep and ask the right questions about why we are the way we are. Once we can pinpoint these reasons, grace can come in, and we can begin to change.

Even though Steve viewed other people as dangerous, he still longed for love, affection, support, and affirmation. So he got married. But it's hard to relate to your spouse when your pattern of coping with emotions is to shut them down.

For the first six or seven years of marriage, Steve and his wife had virtually no emotional connection. Steve had no idea how to have a healthy argument, he knew little about showing true affection, he knew nothing about disagreeing or compromising or saying he was sorry or offering forgiveness—all the healthy emotional give-and-take that good marriages require.

Children came along, and Steve's patterns carried over to his relationship with them. He would come home from work, tired, not wanting to play with his kids. So he would retreat. Steve's pattern of coping was to distance himself from his children— emotionally and physically.

The positive news is that with the help of a trusted group of guys, Steve has been able to make some real progress in the past couple of years. Steve was able to connect with one guy in particular who helped him lift the inner lid to his life. The friend didn't go away, and he challenged Steve to begin to take risks again.

Steve has started to ask himself some serious questions. "How do I engage with my wife and kids? How do I open up emotionally to them? How do I interact?" He's working on this area and making good progress because he's going deeper.

Whenever a situation comes up and Steve is tempted to shut down, he's now able to identify what's happening and break his unhealthy emotional pattern. It's an internal mind-set change. He has to consciously realize that he's not acting appropriately. If he doesn't want to play with his kids because he's tired, he now stops, identifies his fear, and thinks differently: *Who cares if I'm tired? They're only going to be young for so long!* Steve is making a conscious effort to change inner workings that relate outward.

AMONG GOOD COMPANY

When I think of a character in the Bible who consistently let his emotions get ahead of him, I think of the apostle Peter.

We're not told what Peter's family life was like. We're not even sure what his life consisted of until he met Jesus. All we know is that he was a fisherman. He was a man of hard knocks and hard work, familiar with the sea and the wind, not with examining his inner life.

We observe from the Bible's descriptions of Peter that he had a hard time keeping his emotions under control. Maybe he had an aggressive father. Or maybe he never knew his real father and that caused some anger issues in his life. We'll never know. But we do know that when the chips were down, Peter often had a hard time controlling what he said and did.

In the pages of Scripture, he comes across as impetuous.

When Peter sees the Lord walking to him on the water, he jumps overboard and walks on water, too, although his fear soon gets the best of him and he begins to flounder (Matt. 14:28). When Peter, James, and John encounter the transfigured Christ talking with Moses and Elijah, Peter's plan is to grab a hammer and build three houses (Matt. 17:4).

During the night of the Last Supper, Jesus predicts that someone close to Him will betray Him. Immediately, Peter blurts out that he'd never do such a thing. But Christ knows Peter's tendencies, and that night before the rooster crows, Peter does the very thing he swore he'd never do.

I don't believe denying Christ was at the forefront of Peter's heart. Peter just got caught in a difficult situation and allowed his fear to get the best of him. That happens to us on occasion. We get all worked up, we're angry about something, we lose it, and suddenly our emotions are steering the ship. Our adrenaline starts pumping, and we say things we regret and do things we never thought we were capable of.

The funny thing is, shortly before Peter denies Christ, he's prepared to fight to the death for Him. Christ has just finished praying in the Garden of Gethsemane, and a large crowd of soldiers arrives to arrest him. Peter's reaction is to start fighting. He yanks out his sword and slices off a guy's ear (John 18:8–10). Jesus quietly rebukes Peter and then heals the injured man.

You know, few of Peter's last moments with Jesus before the crucifixion were good ones. He wasn't the leader and pillar of the faith that he eventually became. Neither are you and I at times.

We struggle, we miss what God is doing in our lives, and our anger gets out of hand.

The surprising thing is that Christ loves and accepts us no matter what sort of mistakes we make with our emotions. Peter goes on to do amazing things for the Lord. Just read the book of Acts. Peter becomes one of the central figures in building up the early church. Although Peter has made a lot of mistakes, Christ doesn't cross him off the list.

GOD IS ALWAYS WILLING TO PICK UP THE PIECES IN OUR LIVES AND CALL US HIS SON.

That's grace. Grace is always available to us, no matter where we go or what we do. God is always willing to pick up the pieces in our lives and call us His son.

GOOD COMPANY, PART TWO

When I think of another biblical character who blows it emotionally, I think of Jonah. He is the opposite of Peter. Whereas Peter reacts to everything with his fists, Jonah goes the other way. He exhibits emotional vacancy. When the chips are down, he runs and hides.

Can you imagine receiving an audible word from God? I know many men who would give their right arm for that. If it were me I'd be more excited than I had ever been in my life! I'd be more energized, more passionate, more thrilled about the future than ever.

But not Jonah. Right as the first chapter opens, God speaks clear as day to Jonah and what does he do? He takes off running! Can you believe it?!

> The word of the LORD came to Jonah son of Amittai: "Go to the great city of Nineveh and preach against it, because its wickedness has come up before me." But Jonah ran away from the Lord and headed for Tarshish. (Jonah 1:1–3)

Jonah's fear got the best of him, and it kept him from being the man he was truly called to be. This happens to me more times than I like to admit.

When Jonah runs from God, the wind blows on the sea, a violent storm erupts, and the sailors on the ship Jonah is hiding on fear for their lives.

But Jonah still wasn't getting it. He thought that this was his punishment from God because of his disobedience, and that he deserved to die. That's why he announced to the sailors, "I brought this upon you, so go ahead and roll me into the sea and it'll all be over. I'll die, God's anger will be appeased, and everything will be just fine."

So the sailors did what he asked and tossed Jonah into the ocean. But that's not at all what God was doing in this circumstance. It was God's pursuit of Jonah that was causing all of this. And when the sailors threw him overboard, God sent a very unlikely candidate to come to Jonah's rescue—a big fish.

How many crazy experiences do you think have occurred in your life because God was working on your heart? I am sure there have been many times in my own life that something out of the ordinary happened and I blamed the devil, or I blamed the wickedness in somebody else's heart for circumstances in my life that were directed by God.

The lesson here is that the God we serve is always bigger than the circumstances that surround us. He can use anything to get our attention—a fish, a donkey, a whack on the head, a powerful sermon at church—it really doesn't matter. What does matter is that He cares for us and is active in the events that occur in our lives. I'm a firm believer that the sooner we can embrace that reality, the more we will be able to see all of the things God is doing in us every single day.

I love how the Bible describes what happened when Jonah was swallowed by the whale. Here's what it says:

> But the LORD provided a great fish to swallow Jonah, and Jonah
> was inside the fish three days and three nights. (Jonah 1:17)

God *provided* the great fish—I love it! As crazy as it sounds, that's what God did. He was intimately involved in Jonah's entire restoration process.

I'm convinced that God passionately pursues us. He doesn't give up on us, even when we run in the opposite direction from His will. Jonah teaches us that God will go to almost any length to get our attention, to help us, to even allow things that appear to be destructive to occur in order to make us into the men we need to be.

As men, we have been designed in such a way that we are

capable of almost anything we put our minds to. This isn't some crazy New Age idea of living; it's the simple truth of how God has designed us. We are created in God's image. We can accomplish incredible things because God gave us the creative ability to do so.

But our lives can be overwhelmed when we don't know how to handle our emotions—when we either stifle them (like Jonah) or let them rule us (like Peter).

But there is hope. We can be the three-dimensional men we were created to be, men who use all our faculties to think, act, and feel. We can accurately observe our behavior, examine and identify our emotions, and lift the lid on our inner lives to understand what's driving those emotions. With the lid lifted, we can pinpoint the beliefs and experiences behind those emotions that prompt us to act as we do.

And that's where grace can do an amazing work. God doesn't want to leave us stuck in our fear, responding in crazy ways. God's truth can take hold of those core experiences and beliefs and align them with His perfect character. With God's truth at the core of our lives, our emotions can be transformed. We can live the kind of lives we were meant to live.

HOW IT ALL GOES DOWN

We've talked about a lot of heady issues in this chapter, and I hope you've been able to track through what I'm getting at here.

Let me sum up the main themes of this chapter.

We all have emotions, whether we're prone to admit this or not. Our emotions can come out in strange times and ways. For instance, we're driving on the freeway and some jerk cuts us off. We suddenly blow our tops, and then we wonder where the depth of that rage came from. Often we're not quite sure what to do with our feelings.

The problem is that many of our emotions are rooted in fear. Almost any emotion

> WITH GOD'S TRUTH AT THE CORE OF OUR LIVES, OUR EMOTIONS CAN BE TRANSFORMED. WE CAN LIVE THE KIND OF LIVES WE WERE MEANT TO LIVE.

can be traced back to fear. Maybe in the case of being cut off on the freeway, we're afraid of not being respected, or we're afraid of coming in last in some imaginary race, or we're afraid of getting hurt in an accident and not being able to provide for our families. This type of deep inner fear can dominate much in our lives, although we may not realize it's doing so.

Many of our emotions are rooted in fear because we had childhood experiences of trauma, chaos, heartache, disappointment, or friction. These hurtful experiences happened during key formative years. For instance, maybe a bully picked on us and we felt disrespected, or unsafe, or out of control. That same feeling can be what we tap into as adults driving on the freeway when some jerk cuts us off.

We developed our life filters based on our hurtful experiences and our reactions to them. Our life filters carry through to today. We tend to look at all our experiences through the same filters we developed while growing up. For instance, if a bully picked on us when we were young, we developed a certain way of seeing the world that knew bullies could harm us. We avoided them, or perhaps we lashed back at them.

Our emotions emerge (or are hidden) today in relation to our life filters. How we process the world is evidenced in how we react to it. And that's the problem. How we respond to things today is often because we developed patterns and habits of coping in our childhoods. For instance, we respond to the jerk on the freeway using the life filter we created when we were kids and that bully picked on us.

Make sense?

Okay, now we're making progress, but let's not stop here. Let's make this very practical in our own lives.

A Practical Exercise

Ready to do a little work? At this point I invite you to stop and really think through some of these issues we've discussed. Contemplate and meditate on how you have become the person you are today. One of the strong keys to understanding your present is to understand your past. If you can really get a good grip on why you have become the person you are and where your values and beliefs have been shaped from, then you'll have the knowledge that it takes to help create the kind of future you desire and live the way you were truly meant to live.

Work through the questions below alone or with a trusted group of friends.

Pick a moment in your recent past where you had an emotional reaction to something that may have caught you off guard, or you wondered why you did what you did, or perhaps even somebody confronted you about your behavior.

In the space below, simply write down how you acted. All you're doing here is observing your behavior.

Recently, when_____happened,
I responded by _____.

Next, see if you can identify the emotion behind your behavior in that particular experience, and how that particular emotion might relate to that type of deep inner fear.

When that happened, I guess I was feeling _____.
I was probably feeling that way because I fear _____
_____ might happen.

Reach back to a childhood experience where you first felt a similar feeling. Remember how you responded to the experience then, and notice how that experience became part of your life filter. If you're like me, I drew a blank when I got to this point. I had to really think about what happened to me as a child. It's okay if you don't have a lot of information. You may need to chew on this for a few days and get it in your mind before you'll be able to remember. Take your time; the information will come.

When I was a kid, I remember

_____

_____ *happened.*

And I responded then by

_____

_____

_____

_____

So I guess I've grown up believing

_____

_____

_____

_____

Now, take that core belief you formed as a child, the one you just wrote about, and ask yourself what God thinks of that belief. This is where grace really comes in. What Bible verses come to mind that relate to that belief? Through prayer and Scripture, shed new light on what you've always thought was true.

A key verse here is Jeremiah 29:11: "'For I know the plans I have for you,' declares the LORD, 'plans to prosper and not to harm you, plans to give you hope and a future.'"

In other words, God is always a good God. He has a hope

and a plan for your life. Even the traumatic experiences you went through as a kid were part of His plan for you to become who you are today.

Summarize your findings below:

Even though I've grown up believing

_____

_____

_____

I know that Scripture says

_____

_____

_____

Then, based on that new understanding of how to approach your core beliefs, identify a new emotion you might experience whenever a similar experience as you first wrote about comes up. Imagine how your behavior might be different now in times of emotional intensity.

Because God is good, then I can feel

_____

whenever something like

_____ *happens.*

Based on God's truth, I can act

_____.

Basically, what you're doing here is creating a vision of the person you want to be, and what it looks like when you get there.

Once you're able to accomplish this, you can continue to create specific strategies to make progress in a positive direction.

YOUR PLAN TODAY

When it comes to the subject of emotions, no one's asking you to become an emotional basket case. Far from it. Your emotions were given to you by God, and they play an integral role in the strong man God invites you to be.

Emotions can be tricky, but they don't have to rule our lives. Nor do we have to run from them or stuff them down deep inside of us. Emotions are one more component of who we are. With emotions, we are able to live abundantly. We don't need to let fear rule our lives. We can be all God calls us to be.

WE DON'T NEED TO LET
FEAR RULE OUR LIVES.
WE CAN BE ALL GOD
CALLS US TO BE.

REFLECTIONS FOR THOSE WHO CARE
7

T A M M Y   M A L T B Y

Understanding emotions can be tricky; they're hard to understand in ourselves, much less in the lives of others. And sometimes emotions emerge in different ways. For instance, we may think our friend is angry, but he might actually be feeling fearful or guilty or sorrowful.

In open moments, talk to your friend about early experiences in his life. Explore the patterns of coping that he formed at an early age. Discuss the beliefs that may have become rooted in similar behaviors. Always aim to see the truth of a core issue as presented in Scripture. What does the Bible say is truth?

We seldom become true three-dimensional people overnight. Feelings often take time to sort through. This is where our patience with our friend comes into play. Continue to pray that the Lord would heal your friend's feelings.

KEY SCRIPTURE

Set me free from my prison,
that I may praise your name. (Ps. 142:7)

WORD OF GRACE

God is always a good God. He has a hope and a plan for your
life. Even the traumatic experiences you went through as a child
are part of His plan for you. God has no plan B for His children.
In Him, it is always plan A. His is the pathway of redemption.

CHAPTER 8

"I AM SO TICKED OFF"
The Harmful Reality of Anger and Abuse

Pastor Rob was genuinely surprised when Seth didn't show up at staff meeting. Sure, they had exchanged some hard words earlier that morning. Or at least, Pastor Rob had thrown some around—but that was a senior pastor's prerogative, wasn't it? A little argument wasn't enough for a key staff member to skip a meeting. The church was still new. Attendance at every staff meeting was vital for success.

Other staff members settled quickly. The meeting began. Pastor Rob read a short devotional from a leadership book, bounced a prayer off the ceiling, and launched into the week's work.

Pastor Rob knew he had been tough on Seth, but Seth just didn't *get* how difficult church planting was. That's why Rob had really needed to lay into him. Seth insisted on taking days off to be with his family. He had even dared question Rob when Rob regained control of the church finances from the newly formed board (*Those greenhorns just can't handle it yet,* Pastor Rob had concluded). And Seth was so hard to manage—he never seemed to quicken his pace whenever Rob cracked the whip.

Pastor Rob had had no choice but to go postal on him.

"Yes—what is it, Brett? You're interrupting the agenda," Rob said, making little effort to hide the exasperation in his voice. The youth pastor had raised his hand in the middle of the meeting.

"Where do you think Seth went?" Brett said. "I just saw him awhile ago."

"Doesn't matter," snapped Pastor Rob. "He probably went home to take a nap." Rob hoped to get a wry laugh out of that, but none of the associates smiled.

"With all due respect," Brett said, "I know I'm new around here—we all are—but I wonder if it would be a good idea if we all talked about some things before we proceed."

"No time for that," Pastor Rob said. "We need to get on with business. We've got four Easter services to plan by next weekend."

Brett lowered his voice, trying to sound calm yet truthful. "The walls around here aren't that thick. I think everybody could hear the conversation you had with Seth this morning. Some church members were in the building and they heard it too— they asked some pretty tough questions, and I didn't know how to answer. I think it would be good to get this out in the open and talk about how things were handled."

Pastor Rob stood, his face growing crimson. He pointed his finger at Brett and launched in: "Understand this—I'm the senior pastor here. The buck stops with me. Are you the one answering to the network director if we don't bring in the numbers? Is your neck on the line if we lose our funding grant? You have no idea the struggle of a higher calling. We're doing the Lord's work here. In order for this church plant to succeed, it takes all our intensity and passion—absolutely every ounce we can muster. And who are you anyway, to question me? It's nobody's business what I say to another staff member! I am the spiritual authority of this church! You are not in control; I'm in control!" He swatted his cup as he said the last phrase. Hot coffee splattered against the wall. Some splashed on Brett, who frantically tried to wipe off the scalding liquid.

The associates all stared at Pastor Rob. Their faces announced that no one quite knew what to do next.

Pastor Rob glared at each member of the group and shook his head. "You're all pathetic," he said condescendingly. "You call yourself sold out to Christ. None of you really understands what's required of you. You need to give it your all. If you really wanted to make a difference in this church and community, you need to be willing to sacrifice everything—and I do mean everything! This meeting is over."

He stormed out.

* * *

I wish I could tell you that story is unique.

The truth is that far too many "good" Christian work-related interactions, friendships, and family relationships are sources of pain, confusion, and even outright danger.

It happens every day. Christian bosses berate their employees.

Christian husbands smack around their wives. Christian wives abuse their husbands. Christian parents beat or ignore their children. Adult children gouge their parents. Older, stronger brothers and sisters molest younger ones. Christian pastors, teachers, and other authority figures threaten, manipulate, browbeat, or twist God's truth to control their congregations. And churches filled with Christians create climates so filled with hostility, gossip, pressure, and expectations that pastors are forced to resign or endure stress-related illnesses.

Abuse happens—yes, in the lives of Christians too. By "abuse," I don't mean an occasional heated discussion, temper tantrum, impassioned argument, or even infrequent aggressive act—like throwing a remote control against a wall in the midst of a marital skirmish.

I'm talking about a *pattern* of mistreatment. A way of life. Abuse is when one person habitually controls another person to tear that person down. Abuse is when a constant climate of destruction is allowed to fester.

Abuse can take a lot of forms. And pinpointing what exactly constitutes abuse is sometimes tricky.

Abuse might be *physical,* involving actual bodily pain or injury.

It may be *verbal,* involving consistent insults, cruel sarcasm, or put-downs that go far beyond good-natured joking.

ABUSE HAPPENS—YES, IN THE LIVES OF CHRISTIANS TOO.

Abuse may be *psychological,* involving intimidation, mind games, impossible expectations, ill-defined or constantly changing goals, social isolation, forced financial dependence, threats of bodily harm to others or yourself, or acts that elicit fear such as destroying property or hurting pets.

Some abuse is *sexual,* ranging from indecent exposure to coerced sexual acts.

And although we don't hear about it as much, abuse can be *spiritual,* when authority is misused or biblical truths are twisted to justify hurt. Spiritual abuse can come from a pastor, a church leader, a professor, or a church member. It can even come from within the climate created by an organization or institution, or even from a certain neighborhood, town, or region of the country.

It hurts just to talk about it, to think of Christians treating others that way. But if any form of abuse has touched your life, you know the reality is far more hurtful.

You may be an adult victim of childhood abuse. Normal discipline may have turned to vicious beatings. People who were supposed to love you insisted you would never amount to anything. Closeness turned into something sexual and shaming. Sibling rivalry became a campaign of taunting and whispered threats. And though these traumatic events are behind you now, you may still struggle with lingering fear, anger, depression, or feelings of worthlessness.

Perhaps the abuse is not behind you yet.

You may work with a boss or live with a spouse who consistently mistreats you. This abuse may involve regular humiliation, a prolonged climate of hostility, or even slaps and punches. You may walk on eggshells most of the time, never knowing what will set the other person off. Conversation at work or home often may consist of name-calling and put-downs. You may be confused, wondering if what you're experiencing is normal, whether it's really abuse, whether it's really your fault. Perhaps you long to quit work, but you have no idea how you'd support your family. Maybe you fantasize about divorce, but you fear she'd get custody of your kids. Or you want to leave a horrible church situation, but you've grown up there, or you have family and friends there—and what would people think? Or you've become so isolated you have no idea what to think anymore or where to turn. You can't even ask for help because the thought of anyone knowing what your life is like makes you cringe.

There's a chance you may be an abuser.

You're the boss who rules the office with shame and intimidation. You delight in creating situations where no one can win. Or you've lost control at home and discipline your children too harshly. Or you frequently let loose verbally with wounding "zingers." Maybe you hit your wife or girlfriend—you think it's cool, the way men used to slap around women in old movies. Maybe you've done things that scare you or flood you with guilt. . . or simply read the statistics and realized they could apply to you.

If none of these scenarios is true, most probably, you are a witness to abuse.

If you've ever worried about a colleague's management style or your spouse's methods of discipline, or cringed when your grown child's spouse (or your own child) yelled at your grandchild, or worried about the way your daughter's boyfriend treats her, you know how painful such secondhand violence can be. Perhaps as a child you watched one parent beat or bully the other. Perhaps you were aware a sibling was being molested but didn't know what to do.

Even if you're blessed enough to avoid the harsh reality of abuse, chances are it's happening to someone you know. A neighbor. A friend of your children. A colleague or fellow church member. Someone you see every day could be struggling with the destruction, shame, anger, and isolation of being an abused or abusing good Christian guy.

That's the bad news—God's people can do such things to those they claim to love. Good Christian families can endure the trauma of abuse, some of it done in the name of

> EVEN IF YOU'RE BLESSED ENOUGH TO AVOID THE HARSH REALITY OF ABUSE, CHANCES ARE IT'S HAPPENING TO SOMEONE YOU KNOW.

God. It's hard to admit, but this stuff does happen. I can relate. In junior high and high school, I had quite a problem with rage. When people pushed me to the edge by threat or by physical force, everything would suddenly become a blur. I would often "wake up" with blood everywhere, someone's hair in my hands, or on top of some poor sap beating his face in. Yes, I was quite the sweetheart. This rage was stored deep down in my soul. It would emerge in dire circumstances, and once it came barreling out, it seemed like there was nothing I could do to stop it.

Anger isn't exactly the same thing as abuse, but it can be one symptom of it. Left unchecked, anger can build to the place where it explodes from us. I wish I could tell you that rage issues were solely a part of my past. But every now and then they creep back into my life. Just this morning while driving my kids to school, some punk in a sports car zipped in front of me and caused me to slam on my brakes. I'm not sure what it is about driving that can set me over the edge, but it sure does!

Thankfully, I've managed to work through most of my anger issues. But this morning the blood still rushed to my head. I leaned on the horn and kept the pressure on. Then I cut over to the next lane so I could pull alongside him at the next light and give him the nastiest look I could muster. Not real mature, I know, but sometimes this is my reality.

Where do these kinds of intense experiences come from? The types of emotions that lead to damaging patterns of behavior? How can someone get so pushed over the edge he wants to destroy everything and everyone in his path? Why in the world would one person—especially someone who follows Christ—get so riled up that he wants to hurt another person?

ANGER, LEFT UNCHECKED

Like all sin, abuse is a twisted perversion of what God made good. He created us with a need for close relationships. He gives us work and spouses and children and churches and gender roles and even spiritual hierarchies for our support and security and protection. And because we are fallen, because we are wounded, because we are selfish, we inevitably end up misusing these good gifts.

Instead of encouraging each other, we lash out. Instead of

protecting one another, we heap our pain and frustrations on the closest vulnerable person. Instead of building each other up, we desperately try to push ourselves to the top of the heap. Instead of doing what is right, we get it all wrong—and isn't that the very definition of sin?

The issue of *control* is what distinguishes abuse from other sins. Abuse is essentially a power play—an attempt to dominate, manipulate, or coerce another person. This is important to understand because it's so often misunderstood.

You see, abuse isn't an anger issue at its root, although for men, anger is often the primary way abuse is exhibited, and so that's why it's mentioned throughout this chapter. Simply put, abusers act out of a desire or need to control their environment by controlling the people closest to them.

Behind this urge to control, of course, is fear, insecurity, need—a need to feel less vulnerable, to be on top, not to feel pain or loss. People who feel out of control tend to tighten their grip wherever they can and take out their frustration on those who are weaker. Those who have been hurt or wounded attempt to make themselves feel less vulnerable by lashing out against those who can't fight back. And some people . . . well, some people just want to get their own way, no matter what. Sadly, it's human nature for those who fear weakness to prey on those who are even weaker, just as those who have been sinned against will almost always be tempted to sin.

Think you aren't vulnerable to exhibiting abusive behavior? Any behavior can become a pattern if left unchecked. Have you seen these things happen in people you know? Have you ever experienced anything like this yourself?

- Your wife pushes you over the edge and you yell obsceni-
  ties or throw things. Your arguments become fierce and
  frequent. You find yourself looking for a good divorce
  attorney.

- Road rage isn't a video game for you; it's a way of life. Every
  morning's commute is a battle. You visualize ripping the
  head off of the guy who's been tailgating you for the past
  five miles.

- Secretly, you like the feeling you get when you "lay into
  somebody" at work. Everyone walks on pins and needles
  because they don't want to set you off.

- You totally freak out at the referee at your son's basketball
  game. Why won't that jerk call a foul on the opposing team?!

- You're frustrated because your wife doesn't act the way you
  think a wife is supposed to act. It's your responsibility as
  head of the home to control everything that goes on and
  enforce that by any means necessary. That's what the Bible
  says—doesn't it?

- Your pastor has been preaching some real duds lately. You
  withhold your tithe for a while, just to put pressure on.
  You call up some of your buddies and start talking about
  getting him fired. You're the one to do it too—you carry
  some real weight around your church.

- Your daughter's thirteen now and really filling out. Ever
  since she was a little girl, you've always kissed her goodnight
  on the lips. Lately the kisses have been just a little too long.

- Let's face it, your son isn't the brightest kid on the block.
  The kid can't do anything right. You let him know that

too—regularly. But whenever you call him *stupid* or *idiot*, it's just teasing, isn't it?

- You've been dating a woman for a while now and like to leave gifts for her at her home and work. You hate it when she spends time with other people. She's asked you not to call so often, leave so many gifts, or spend so much time with her, but you don't respect her requests. She'll come around one of these days, won't she?

- You routinely share all your personal struggles with your fourteen-year-old son and tell him you don't know what you would do without him.

- You consistently promise things to your son or daughter but never follow through.

- You think your wife is lazy because she doesn't work outside of the home. When she gets a job, you tell her it's "not a real job" because she's not earning enough money to really help. When she tries to go back to college, you tell her she's selfish for expecting you to support her while she's in school.

Like I said, getting an exact bead on the definition of *abuse* can be tricky. Any mention of the word *abuse* can easily become a sensitive and highly charged topic of discussion. But in its essence, abuse is a pattern of harming another person. It's the pervasive, willful use of power to control (or neglect) others.

It may be somewhat difficult to find out exactly where the behavior of abuse comes from, especially in men. I believe it comes from three primary areas.

How a Man Grew Up

How you were raised as a child has so much to do with how you act as an adult.

I remember very clearly how rage-filled my home was growing up. I honestly don't think there was a day that went by when someone didn't blow up. Constant screaming, yelling, and cussing were the routine recipes of the day.

What did it teach me as a kid? Simple. When something's not going the way you want it to go, you explode—you make sure everyone knows how ticked off you are. You insult everyone in sight. You escalate the violence by throwing things around the room or punching whoever is within arm's length, then jump in your car and screech the tires as you drive off.

It's very easy for the behaviors you see modeled as a child to become patterns in your adult life. You can't imagine any other way to live. You imitate what's been shown to you.

How a Man Is Wired

"How you're wired" means how your personality is predisposed to respond to stressful situations. Typically, there are two responses: fight or flight.

"Fight" means that when a stressful situation comes your way, you take off your gloves and start swinging. You yell, hit, scream, escalate.

"Flight" means you tend to run from conflict. You shut

down emotionally. You might stuff your emotions. You might seek to physically distance yourself from the stress. Sometimes all that bottled stress can build to the place where it spews out at once.

Neither the "fight" nor "flight" responses are wrong, in and of themselves. Yet because of our propensity to sin, abuse can result when either response is left unchecked. A "fighter" can become a physical, verbal, or sexual abuser, or respond in anger and rage if abuse has been done to him. I think this is one of the biggest challenges I've personally had to work through. A "flighter" can become more of an emotional abuser, someone who controls through manipulation. Or a flighter can simply collapse in on himself—if abuse has been done to him, he may just clam up and implode.

Interestingly, Jesus modeled us a third way to respond to stress, one that was neither fight nor flight. It was to stand strong and hold out for truth while avoiding revenge and retaliation. Think of His cleansing the temple or standing up to the lawyers and Pharisees who tested Him. He taught us to forgive abuse, but not to give in to it. To be salt and light, not punching bags.

And even though Christ challenged us to have so much love we would give up our lives for our friends (John 15:13) or for the sake of the gospel (Mark 10:29), He never suggested we should give up our lives for the sake of someone else's power trip. He certainly never called us to save anyone through our sacrifice. Dying for someone's sins is His job, and He's already taken care of that!

HOW A MAN SEES HIMSELF

How you see value in yourself comes out in every aspect of your life. If you see yourself as worthless, you tend to respond accordingly. Or if you've been extremely hurt, it can be easy to hit back.

As the old saying goes, "Hurt people hurt people"—with the first "hurt" an adjective describing the person, and the second a verb, describing the action that can result.

> HOW YOU SEE VALUE IN YOURSELF COMES OUT IN EVERY ASPECT OF YOUR LIFE.

If you've been abused in some way, it's easy to view yourself as "lesser" than something else. This feeling can turn around and exhibit itself in abusive behavior. Abuse is really a cry for security or significance, acceptance, and support.

But abuse is never the answer, even when a person has been so hurt he now sees the world as something so painful it has to be controlled at all costs. Abuse has serious consequences. Even when abuse is not fatal—and it can be!—it ruins lives and destroys souls. It can truly desolate an individual or a family, and the conflict it generates is readily passed from one generation to another.

Many men never learn this, and it costs them dearly. Just like it did for Jared.

FILLED WITH RAGE

Jared still remembers how sore his knees felt, crouching in the closet for close to five hours with his little brother by his side.

Down below in the living room, a battle raged. Jared's mother and father were hard at it, hammer and tongs. Plates flew, lamps crashed over, punches and slaps could be heard, screams resonated through the night.

It wasn't an unusual incident—it just seemed that particular night went on longer than most. Violence was a consistent part of Jared's childhood. From his earliest memories, anger was the routine way of dealing with problems. It's how his parents and grandparents responded to any stressful situation. Many days, Jared's household turned into a boxing ring. Fistfights, slapping faces, throwing things around the room—these were consistent methods of dealing with things a person didn't like.

As Jared grew older, those same patterns became ingrained in him. It seemed like no matter how much he cared for someone or something, his rage would end up wrecking everything. He had trouble making and keeping friends. He was kicked off his school's soccer team for blowing up at his coach. He quit going to youth group because his youth pastor told him he couldn't bring his car to church anymore (once, in a fit of rage, he tore out of the parking lot, sending gravel everywhere).

This issue came out even worse, soon after he was married.

Jared and his new wife had experienced their share of disagreements throughout their dating life, but their first serious fight came on the day after coming home from their honeymoon. It was over something stupid—where to store the china they had received as a wedding gift. Jared remembers wondering why his wife was being so unreasonable. He remembers ripping open boxes, throwing plates everywhere. He remembers the look on his wife's face when a plate sailed into their sliding-glass door, smashing the plate and cracking the door. He remembers slamming his car door and stomping on the accelerator.

That was all he remembers until two hours later when a police car pulled him over. Cost: a $259 speeding ticket. Plus $800 worth of china that he had wrecked. Plus more than $1,000 for a new sliding door. All in all, a pretty expensive argument. Not to mention the damage it did to the relationship.

The most frustrating thing to Jared was that he couldn't seem to control his anger. He would flare up at the smallest set of circumstances. He didn't feel like he asked much of his wife— just that the house would be clean when he came home from work. One day it wasn't, and he dumped the contents of the vacuum bag all over the carpet. Another time, an old friend from his wife's past called—not a boyfriend, just a guy she had worked with on youth staff at a church—to say congrats on getting married, and Jared ripped the phone off the wall. Once, Jared's wife came home an hour after she said she would (she "just lost track of time" at the mall, she said), and Jared grabbed her purse and destroyed all her makeup (so she "wouldn't look like a whore" and attract so much attention, he said).

About two years into their marriage, things took a sharp turn for the worse. No one even remembers what the argument was about now. But Jared's hand came up so fast there was no time to think. *Whack!* Right across the face, knocking her to the ground. She told people at church she bumped her cheek while cleaning the oven.

His wife had some anger issues too. But this was no excuse for Jared's bad behavior. Abuse is never a victim's fault, even if the victim makes mistakes or acts badly. This is so important to recognize because blaming a victim is a common tactic for rationalizing abuse. "If you just kept the house better," a husband may claim, "I wouldn't have to get rough with you." Or a parent may tell a child, "It's your fault I hit you—you wouldn't behave."

One night, Jared and his wife totally got into it. Insults escalated into threats. He said she better watch it or he'd hit her again. She slapped him first, then kicked him in the shins before he had time to react.

Jared's rage rose up. This time, he smacked her in the jaw, knocking her across the floor. He was so angry he couldn't even see straight. He grabbed her by the hair, dragged her to the front door, and threw her outside. He locked the door, then turned to the wall, punching holes in the sheet rock repeatedly.

She spent the night at a friend's house that night, then came home after he apologized, but things were never the same. One dreadful night another argument ensued. Angry and out of control, Jared picked up an end table and threw it across the room. His wife stepped in front of the table at just the wrong moment, and it hit her in the head. Blood gushed everywhere. Jared rushed her to the hospital. The result? Twenty-three stitches in her forehead. Jared couldn't believe his anger had gotten so out of control.

Abuse is a legal issue as well as a social one, and the police showed up at the hospital to question Jared. Jared spent the night in jail, charged with spousal abuse. That was the rock-bottom place that shook him into action. While in lockup, Jared got on his knees and cried out for God to save him—to save them both . . . to save their marriage, their lives, their hopes, their future.

And God met him there.

His wife dropped the charges.

Jared began going to counseling.

His wife began an intensive discipleship program with an older woman in their church.

Jared began meeting regularly with a small group of trusted guys for accountability and support.

Today, the issue isn't totally resolved, but Jared and his wife are in process. There have been no more outbursts of physical violence. Jared and his wife are still together, learning how to love and live together and work things out and even disagree peacefully. He's beginning to have the courage to face some of the core issues that brought him to this place. She's going through her own transformation and healing process. There is definitely still a journey ahead of them, but they are well underway.

An Abusive King

Abuse is nothing new. Families, friends, and business colleagues have been hurting each other throughout history. Some of the most prominent families and relationships in biblical history experienced episodes of horrid abuse.

King Saul found himself in such a predicament. He had always had a bit of a self-image issue. When he was first anointed king by the prophet Samuel, Saul complained to him that he was just a nobody—"from the smallest tribe of Israel," from "the least of all the clans of the tribe of Benjamin" (1 Sam. 9:21).

Saul tried. He faithfully led the Israelites into battle against their enemies. But one fighting season when a giant named Goliath showed up, Saul preferred to remain in his tent, strategizing about what could be done to defeat this huge menace. Ever wonder why David, the shepherd boy, fought Goliath? Shouldn't it have been King Saul who led the charge?

Surely Saul felt that. When the throngs of admirers cheered David's victories instead of his, Saul's jealousy began to burn. David was his friend, someone who looked up to him, his son-in-law, a valiant man in his army, but Saul just couldn't handle the connection. He both loved David and hated him—a classic breeding ground for abuse.

One day when David didn't show up to dinner at the king's table, Saul snapped. Scripture records the story in 1 Samuel 20:27–33. In this case, Saul didn't harm David directly, but his tendency toward abuse was exhibited in the behavior he demonstrated toward his own son, Jonathan.

> Then Saul said to his son Jonathan, "Why hasn't the son of Jesse come to the meal, either yesterday or today?"
> Jonathan answered, "David earnestly asked me for permission

to go to Bethlehem. He said, 'Let me go, because our family is observing a sacrifice in the town and my brother has ordered me to be there. If I have found favor in your eyes, let me get away to see my brothers.' That is why he has not come to the king's table."

Saul's anger flared up at Jonathan and he said to him, "You son of a perverse and rebellious woman! Don't I know that you have sided with the son of Jesse to your own shame and to the shame of the mother who bore you? As long as the son of Jesse lives on this earth, neither you nor your kingdom will be established. Now send and bring him to me, for he must die!"

"Why should he be put to death? What has he done?" Jonathan asked his father.

But Saul hurled his spear at him to kill him. Then Jonathan knew that his father intended to kill David.

An abusive pattern was set in motion. And forever after, Saul's only intent was to harm David.

Before we judge Saul too harshly, I think we might find some of the same tendencies in our own lives if we lift the inner lid to our hearts. The roots of abuse often lie closer to the surface than we think. Perhaps we are not so different from Saul in the end.

- Have you ever felt jealousy for someone who always seems to have a leg up on you?
- Ever found it impossible to forgive someone or overlook his faults?

- Ever been so angry you imagine inflicting harm on a person?

It's when times are difficult that we find out what is really in our heart. It's when we're stressed, tired, annoyed, lonely, or fearful that our true character emerges. We can't hide it then. Saul slowly but surely revealed his true colors. The rage he was always trying to control boiled inside him until he couldn't contain it any longer. Soon after the spear-throwing incident, Saul went on an insane tirade, murdered many of the priests of God, consulted a witch for guidance, and finally died.

What caused him to exhibit such anger? Some of us have read over that passage so many times it's become commonplace to us—but think about it: Saul's anger reached the point where he hurled his spear at his own son to kill him!

The truth about the issues of bitterness, resentment, jealousy, and envy is that they never remain stagnant in our lives. They never remain neutral. Unless checked, they grow and fester until they explode into rage. And rage can become abuse. That's why, as men, it's so important we work through the issues that seethe beneath the surface of our lives. It's so important that we extend forgiveness and remove jealousy so that it doesn't grow to the point where we can't control it anymore.

Because in the end, anger will destroy us, just like it did Saul.

As with Saul, so it is with us, a problem with wrath can lead you to harm the object of your wrath and anyone else who gets in the way. A number of good Christian guys have hurt their wives and children because their anger went unchecked. The devastation of angry words and angry attitudes can be long-lasting. Children are scarred for life and will likely have the same trouble with anger and rage that they have seen in their fathers.

I want to make it clear that not all anger is wrong. The Bible talks about two forms of anger. There's destructive anger, directed at inflicting harm on other people. This kind of anger grows and seeks release in such a way that it is not satisfied until it has harmed another person.

Then there's godly anger or righteous indignation. This type of anger is not wrong. In fact, as men, this type of anger can fuel us to do courageous acts.

For example, one of the issues in our world I'm absolutely incensed about is the plight of orphans. To hear about a little girl in a Russian orphanage who is repeatedly sexually abused by the orphanage caretaker makes me furious. Or to hear about another child who "graduated" from an orphanage at age fifteen simply because there was no more room for her, and to know that without continued education and support she'll have a 60 percent chance of turning to prostitution just so she can eat—that almost drives me insane!

With this type of anger, I don't want to hurt someone. I want to help someone. This type of anger drives me to action.

Because of my righteous indignation, this is an area I invest much of my time and my resources in. I take trips to Russia with my friends, business associates, and pastors so we can implement programs that stop this kind of abuse from happening.

When Jesus exhibited anger, it was the perfect kind of anger.

His anger always led to a positive result. Matthew 21:12–14 records one such incident:

> Jesus entered the temple area and drove out all who were buying and selling there. He overturned the tables of the money changers and the benches of those selling doves. "It is written," he said to them, "My house will be called a house of prayer, but you are making it a 'den of robbers.'"

Do you catch the seriousness of this action? Jesus actually picked people up by the scruff of the neck and threw them out of the temple. These people were stealing from others and taking advantage of the poor. Christ was angry because none of these moneychangers had any concern or respect for God.

This isn't the only place you see Jesus indignant. Mark 3:1–6 records another story:

> Another time he went into the synagogue, and a man with a shriveled hand was there. Some of them were looking for a reason to accuse Jesus, so they watched him closely to see if he would heal him on the Sabbath. Jesus said to the man with the shriveled hand, "Stand up in front of everyone."
>
> Then Jesus asked them, "Which is lawful on the Sabbath: to do good or to do evil, to save life or to kill?" But they remained silent.
>
> He looked around at them in anger and, deeply distressed at their stubborn hearts, said to the man, "Stretch out your hand." He stretched it out, and his hand was completely

restored. Then the Pharisees went out and began to plot with the Herodians how they might kill Jesus.

There are several things in this passage that led to Jesus's anger. One was that the so-called rulers of the law had no compassion for those who were suffering. They were more concerned about Jesus' following a strict set of impossible rules than they were about a person who needed help.

Second, Christ was appalled at the fact that their hearts had become so hard. Hard-hearted people are not who human beings were created to be. We were created to love God with our whole hearts and our neighbors as ourselves.

Of course none of us can claim to act in exactly the same fashion that Jesus acted. We are not perfect in any sense of the word, but we can learn to live by channeling our anger toward righteousness, not unrighteousness.

A NEXT STEP

If anger is not righteous anger, it can lead to abuse. And abuse can happen to anyone, not just to the weak or the poor or the unchurched. It can ruin the lives of kings or servants. Smart, strong, resourceful people can be abused and become abusers. Christians are no exception to this rule. The only real qualification for becoming acquainted with abuse is being human.

Here's another thing to note: only rarely can abuse continue over any length of time without an enabler of some kind—a friend, a family member, a pastor or teacher—who knows or suspects what is going on but does nothing to stop it.

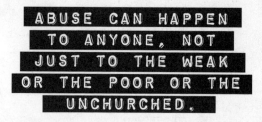

ABUSE CAN HAPPEN TO ANYONE, NOT JUST TO THE WEAK OR THE POOR OR THE UNCHURCHED.

A given situation, in fact, may have more than one enabler—some fearful, some busy or distracted, some unsure what to do, some simply uncaring. And every good Christian guy is in danger of filling this role at one time or another. Anytime we give glib or shallow advice to someone who is hurting, every time we notice a harsh word or a bruise but decide it's none of our business, every time we decide not to call a friend who has become defiant and unyielding, we could be helping an abuser continue his or her reign of terror.

Does this mean we should all commit ourselves to rescuing abuse victims? Not necessarily. Without specific training and support, we can end up not only causing further harm, but actually endangering ourselves and others. Yet I believe there are times when the Lord may bring an abuse situation to our attention specifically so that we can be catalysts for change in that situation. At the very least, we can act as a friend. We can listen and pray and research sources of professional help.

God never rates loyalty higher than truth. He never ranks a human relationship higher than following Him or obeying His will. And when relationships break, when we continually fail each other, when we just can't live together in love and integrity, when one person insists on abusing another, God often provides a way of escape, a way to build a new life. In such cases even the breakup of a family, job, church, or institution—though tragic—can be seen as an act of mercy and grace.

It's not my intention in this chapter to offer a step-by-step formula for overcoming abuse. Honestly, that is beyond the scope of my training, and it's also beyond the scope of this book. Rather, I hope that in this chapter you can learn to recognize some of the signs of abuse and accurately determine if you are being abused or if you are being an abuser. What comes first is truth—naming the abuse for what it is, without excuses or cover-ups.

What happens then?

If you are being abused, make your family's safety the top priority. If you are habitually being kicked around, for instance at a job, this will only build in your life and spill out in other areas—this usually means your wife and kids will feel the brunt of your hurt. That's not fair to you and it's not fair to them. Do whatever is necessary to stop the abuse and break the cycle, even if it means quitting your job and selling your house.

If you are an abuser, seek professional help. This is an issue greater than something you can work through on your own.

There will almost certainly need to be a period of healing and restoration for a victim, a time when the abuser works through old issues and learns new ways of living with others. And forgiveness will almost certainly play a part in this healing, but it may take awhile, and forgiveness won't necessarily mean restoring the relationship. Reconciliation can only follow true repentance—which involves real change over a period of time and a slow rebuilding of trust.

Keep in mind that repentance is not the same thing as remorse. It's common for abusers to feel remorse, apologize profusely to those they have hurt, and have sincere intentions for change—only to fall back into the abusive behavior. As with an addiction, the best intentions are often not enough—even when abusers claim that God has changed them. That's not to say abusers *can't* change, but it rarely happens easily or quickly. The process involves true repentance and a deep commitment to stop all abusive behavior. It also requires the help and support of other people, the establishment of new patterns and habits, and—I believe—an ongoing, supernatural infusion of grace.

Only time will confirm that change is both real and lasting. Only time will show that reconciliation is really possible. But even if an abuser never repents, God's grace can still work at transforming an abusive situation.

GRACE FOR TODAY

How does grace fit into all this?

We've learned anger is a very touchy emotion. Channeled in the right direction, it can help us act on our compassion, make a right where others have wronged, and institute biblical justice where there is injustice.

But fleshly anger allowed to go unchecked can cause serious destruction in our own lives and the lives of those closest to us.

As good Christian men, we all walk in our own form of brokenness. The point of this chapter or any of the chapters we've discussed is not to expect any of us to be absolutely perfect. It does mean, however, that as we walk in grace we agree to walk in integrity and deal with the issues that continue to be struggles in our lives. Responsibility always begins with us. Our focus is not being perfect but walking toward wholeness—to walk toward a God who always has His arms wide open to us no matter what we've done. We do this by walking in truth, allowing a few other trusted men in our lives from whom we hold no secrets, and confessing our weaknesses before a God who loves us and is quick to forgive us.

The older I get, the more thankful I am that this is the kind of God we serve. I need to continually remind myself that He is not in heaven with a hammer cocked behind His ear waiting to pummel me when I screw up—quite the opposite. Those were lies I used to believe about God. What has really helped set me free is to know about God's grace and mercy.

One of my favorite psalms describes so perfectly what we need to know about God's true heart and character. This gives us the confidence we need to come into His presence no matter how many times we sin:

The LORD is compassionate and gracious,
slow to anger, abounding in love. (Ps. 103:8)

If abuse is part of your life, please take the courageous steps you know you need to take. Deal with your pain. Deal with the personal disappointment and shame. Be willing to be honest with a group of trusted men. Step up and let God teach you how to use your anger in productive ways. Be the real man God has called you to be.

God does not hate you. He hears your prayers when you call out to Him. And He is working right now in your life for your good.

A brighter future won't happen automatically. It might not happen the way you think or turn out the way you would have chosen.

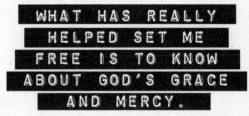

WHAT HAS REALLY HELPED SET ME FREE IS TO KNOW ABOUT GOD'S GRACE AND MERCY.

You will need to seek help and make some hard choices. You may have some times when desolation seems to stalk you, when the wilderness stretches wide before you.

But there is a future for you. You *will* see the God who sees you. And this God will help you face even the most dark and shameful things you have done and the things that have been done against you.

In this God, there is always hope. That's the message of grace.

REFLECTIONS FOR THOSE WHO CARE
8

T A M M Y   M A L T B Y

If you suspect someone you know is an abuser or a victim of abuse, what do you do? Many of us have grown up believing we should not get involved in other people's business—and indeed we should be careful when it comes to sticking our noses where they don't belong.

But abuse falls into a different category. Abuse can do serious harm—even kill—people we care about. It's a legal issue as much as a social one. And if we suspect someone we know is an abuser or a victim of abuse, we have a responsibility to become involved. These are our brothers in the Lord who are dangerously straying, our sisters in Christ who are being hurt, our friends and our family in harm's way.

For either the abuser or the abused, the bottom-line message is this: *get help*.

When people have been sinned against, they often find themselves sinning in the same way. Encourage people in this situation to take whatever steps are necessary. Get the woman to safety. Get the man to counseling. Do the work necessary to break the cycle. There is hope. There can be healing, but only when the problem is identified can the problem be healed.

KEY SCRIPTURE

Carry each other's burdens, and in this way you will fulfill the law of Christ. (Gal. 6:2)

WORD OF GRACE

God will help you face the most dark and shameful things you have done and the things that have been done against you. There is always hope in God. That's the message of grace.

CHAPTER 9

"I WANT TO GIVE UP"
The Weary Grind of Long-Term Discouragement

Hugh pulled his old sedan to the side of the road and slammed the door behind him. The state park felt cold and isolated. Winter sunlight barely peeked through the clouds. Grass beneath his feet looked dead and colorless.

Hugh had come to the park to think. He had left work without clocking out—he knew he should return soon, but he simply had to get away. Try as he might, he couldn't stomach the thought of enduring one more minute at a job he hated.

When the economy had bottomed out and Hugh had lost his "real" job, he had taken a position in another company, several rungs down, as a stop-gap measure. It paid the bills and kept his family in their house, but the job felt completely dead-end. There were no promotion possibilities, no creative opportunities, no appreciative gestures, no incentives—just a dingy cubicle, an old phone, endless cold-call lists, and a supervisor who should never have been promoted to her position. For Hugh, every day meant working as hard as he could for a paycheck that barely kept his family afloat.

Hugh had desperately sought other jobs. Lots of jobs. He had networked and devoured books and attended seminars and upped his job placement skills. Over the past four years he had mailed out more than two hundred résumés. Interviews came and went—he had shone on many of them. But for some reason, none of the other jobs panned out. Over time, the stop-gap job had grown to feel like his destiny. Hugh felt trapped, hemmed in, hopeless, and helpless. There was no going forward, no going back. He was sure he would be chained to his tiny cubicle for the rest of his life.

Hugh visited the park often. Normally it was a family-friendly recreational area with waterfalls that cascaded over a ravine. Hugh hiked to the lookout point and peered over the railing at the rocks underneath the falls. All around Hugh was a sense of darkness he couldn't throw off. His mind felt shaky. He felt like a slave, completely trapped in his circumstances, yearning for release but unable to break free.

How easy it would be, he thought, *to just step over the railing and never come back. It would look like an accident. No one would ever know . . .*

Have you ever been there?

Perhaps there is one area of your life that hems you in. That struggle has been a long-term factor, and it's not getting any better. You don't see a solution ahead. All you see is the struggle, and that one dark area now feels inescapable. You've convinced yourself you will not overcome it. You cannot rid yourself of the sense of overpowering dread it brings to your life. All you can do—all you *must* do—is keep yourself on the park side of the railing, get back in your sedan, and drive back to a job you hate.

That's what Hugh did.

In body anyway.

His heart, his spirit, his motivation, his optimism—all took the plunge. The only hope he could imagine lay in the false release of a long jump over a railing.

If the struggle I've just described sounds familiar to your situation, this chapter is for you.

This chapter is different from the others because it doesn't focus on a particular area of brokenness. Instead, it's a chapter about enduring pressure over time. A certain long-term broken-ness comes when that happens and threatens to carry us beyond our endurance and understanding. When problems don't get solved, suffering doesn't go away, difficulties aren't untangled, habits aren't broken, loved ones keep hurting us, then despera-tion and weariness set in.

It's about those times when we've prayed and fasted and tried harder and waited on the Lord and rolled up our sleeves and taken action and read books and taken extra classes and gone to seminars and networked and shifted paradigms and looked out of the box and colored outside of the lines and done everything we know to do . . . and our circumstances still don't improve. Sometimes, they even get worse.

I know many good Christian guys like my friend Hugh, men who have struggled for years with discouragement. Sometimes their tough situations exist through no fault of their own, like the economy falling out. At other times, their long-term pain is a consequence of sin—either their own or the sin of others.

Regardless, the pain of these men is chronic, their disappointment deep. Every season of hope seems to be followed by another season of trouble that's the same as before, even worse than before. Their prayers echo the words of Psalm 13:1–2:

> How long, O LORD? Will you forget me forever?
> How long will you hide your face from me?
> How long must I wrestle with my thoughts
> and every day have sorrow in my heart?
> How long will my enemy triumph over me?

When I think of long-term discouragement, I think of my friend Ken, who played Triple A baseball in his first years after college. He's been in a wheelchair for years ever since multiple sclerosis fried his nerve endings.

Or Bill, whose adult son has been in and out of rehab more times than anyone can remember.

Or Jack, who lost custody of his four young children after his divorce. His ex-wife married another guy and they moved three states away. Jack has visitation rights every other weekend, but it's pretty hard to make that trip more than a few times a year.

Or Russell, who wonders if he'll ever find victory from the cravings of porn.

Or Dave, who's been a senior pastor his whole life. At age

sixty-one, he just resigned from an impossible church situation. He's burned out, hurt, frustrated, but doesn't have the finances yet to retire. He's got to find one last job. Pastoring is all he's ever known.

Or Elliot, whose wife is an alcoholic.

Or Dan, whose wife is chronically depressed.

Or Trent, a single guy who longs to be married. The temptation is always there to fool around, but Trent believes sexual purity is the way to go. Still . . . he's in his midthirties, and that's a long time to keep in check.

WHAT DO YOU DO WHEN YOU'RE IN A WILDERNESS OF PAIN WITH NO END IN SIGHT?

Or Ted, who suffered permanent brain damage from a car accident a few years ago. He functions quite well, but his short-term memory is shot. Ask him to meet for lunch and he has to write it down. If something's not on his notepad, it doesn't exist anymore.

I believe that these guys, in their most honest moments, are simply asking themselves—or the Lord, "Will I ever feel good again?"

Where is God in times like these?

If we want to talk about real grace, about the love of the Father, about God's offerings to us in our brokenness, I think we have to ask that question. We need to ask how good Christian guys can survive these times of extended suffering without stepping over the railing and plunging to the rocks below.

What do you do when you're in a wilderness of pain with no end in sight?

What do you do when you wake up in the morning and say to yourself, "I feel like giving up"?

THE TAIL END OF A SHEEP HERD

Twenty years.

Could it really be twenty years?

Jacob added it up: seven years of labor for Leah, seven for Rachel, and six years of labor for the flocks.

It had been two solid decades out in the fields cleaning up behind the ends of sheep. Twenty years of bottom-rung work—and there was no end in sight. To top it off, Jacob's boss, Laban, had changed Jacob's wages ten times during those years.

Can you hear the sigh of a discouraged man?

I just want to give up.

What was the promise that God had made to Jacob—years ago, back when he had fled from his brother Esau's wrath and headed toward Laban's house?

The promise unfolded like this: one dusty evening as Jacob traveled through the desert, he had wrapped his cloak about him, slipped a stone under his head for a pillow, and God appeared to him in a dream. Angels ascended and descended to heaven in the dream, and God declared, "I will give you and your descendants the land on which you are lying. Your descendants will be like the dust of the earth, and you will spread out to the west and to the east, to the north and to the south" (Gen. 28:13–14). That was the promise: God was going to bless Jacob greatly someday.

But twenty years caring for sheep hardly seemed like Jacob was on the right road.

Sure, the years had started brightly enough. Jacob's initial motivation was marriage to the woman he loved. Rachel had it all—eyes, hair, smile—the seven years Jacob worked for her felt like only a few days. The night of their wedding seemed like a dream. At last, the bride Jacob loved was his! Music and celebration earmarked the event, and when it was all over the lights were low, the honeymoon tent was dark, and all felt perfect. One problem: the morning after the wedding, there was the older sister, Leah, naked in Jacob's bed.

Where was Rachel?!

"It's not our custom to have a younger sister married before an older one," said Laban with a raised eyebrow, when Jacob complained. Jacob was tricked, deceived, held to his bottom-rung position.

Rachel was given to Jacob a week later as a concession, but much of the joy was already gone by then. The happy family Jacob had once dreamed about had a wrench thrown in it now. The new deal meant Jacob had to work another seven years for Rachel, but his discouragement came from something greater than more work. His two wives, Leah and Rachel, quarreled constantly. Rachel felt loved, but she couldn't have any children. Leah felt unloved, but she had no problem cranking out the kids. Tension grew in Jacob's family and wouldn't quit.

Then there was the trouble over the herds—the real wealth

of the era in that part of the world. Laban had not offered any wages to Jacob besides brides, so Jacob cut him a hard deal. Eventually Laban agreed to let Jacob have all his spotted and speckled animals, but tension mounted there too. Jacob's herds increased while Laban's didn't, and soon Laban's sons complained that Jacob had stolen all their father's wealth. Jacob noticed Laban's attitude toward him was not what it had been, but Jacob just kept working. The heat consumed him in the daytime and the cold at night. Sleep fled from his eyes. It was a life of toil, hardship, and tension. And after twenty years, Jacob had had enough.

True—part of Jacob's weariness and desperation was brought on by his own sin. Jacob was a man of deception, trickery, and duplicity, and it came around to bite him. But part of Jacob's struggle was brought on by the sin of others—whatever lying Jacob had done, others had cheated him and lied to him too. His struggle had taken too long. There was no solution in sight.

Twenty years in the wilderness.

If God didn't act soon, another twenty years would pass. More tension. More hardship. Another twenty would pass after that. And another twenty after that. Can you hear Jacob's cry? "God, I'm so tired of my circumstances. God, help. I'm weary and worn. God, why don't You change things? God, move me out of this!"

This is the cry of anyone suffering from long-term discouragement. When our hardships don't change, we feel hopeless, isolated, abandoned, rejected, lonely, vulnerable, cheated, misunderstood, and just plain weary. Jacob's cry is the cry all good Christian guys feel in the midst of long-term struggle. *God, just get me out of here!*

The struggle is particularly hard if someone else's sin or shortcomings put us in this place. We did the right thing. We provided. We tithed. We stuck around and helped out when no one would. We said the courteous

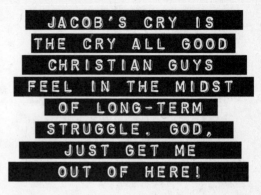

JACOB'S CRY IS THE CRY ALL GOOD CHRISTIAN GUYS FEEL IN THE MIDST OF LONG-TERM STRUGGLE. GOD, JUST GET ME OUT OF HERE!

thing. We kept our nose clean. But in the end we didn't get what we deserved. We expected chocolate cake and got a bran muffin. Where is the blessing? Where is the reward for faithfulness? If we do the right thing, won't God bless us? Isn't that the exchange?

Long-term discouragement can feel like being in a crowd of people at the end of a long day in Disneyland when everybody's headed for their cars. It doesn't matter if you have a plan to leave more quickly; you're at the mercy of the crowd. You're hemmed in, stuck. You can walk only when they walk. Try as you might, you can't get ahead of the crowd. Sure, you can vent your frustration. You can struggle and strive to push through. But in the end, you only move when someone else wants you to move. You're confined—and that's never comfortable. There is simply no way you can reach your destination any faster. Sometimes it feels like you'll never reach your destination at all.

The real shock is that sometimes God is doing the confining. Psalm 139:5 says that God hems us in. What sort of consolation is there from knowing that God might be behind the circumstances of our long-term discouragement?

He might not have caused the circumstances, but He definitely allowed them.

In fact, He might not even want us to get ourselves out of our difficult situation.

Why would a good God do such a thing?!

Why God—*why?!*

My friend Joey has asked this question.

WHEN YOU FEEL LIKE YOU'RE GOING UNDER

Joey had been whispering that question silently to himself for years. One day in a movie theater he asked it out loud. He remembers watching the screen, drawing a direct parallel between what he saw and his life: The wound on the screen was fatal. When the *Titanic* hit the iceberg, the ship ripped open. The vessel once deemed "unsinkable" was going under, fast.

Too many people. Too few lifeboats. There were no alternatives. Only one courageous choice could be made: the men aboard the *Titanic* would sacrifice themselves. "Women and children first!" the men called out. The men would drown so that others might live. The cry, "Men first!" would never be heard. These were men of honor. They did what they knew was true.

As Joey watched the movie, he began to cry. Not just a sniffle either; he began to sob.

In the darkened theater, he realized what he was doing and almost laughed at himself—here he was, crying over the *Titanic*. It didn't seem very macho.

But as he sorted out his thoughts, he knew it wasn't the movie he was crying over. He had never cried like this before in his life. A hidden truth was surfacing, and Joey was beginning to face it.

The men on the *Titanic* had *decided* to die.

That was his reality too. Like an erupting volcano, Joey could not hold back the lava of emotion, and he could not cease his sobbing.

Joey's wife, Sharon, had been ill for virtually all of their twenty years of marriage. Sadly, only for the first three months of their married life had she been healthy. Her sickness was serious. During one period of their two decades of marriage, she had been hospitalized for six years. She had to be under unique care in another state. Month after month, Joey flew to where Sharon rehabilitated.

There had been one consolation during those twenty years: medical insurance had covered most of the astronomical hospital expenses. But that coverage was now ending, and Joey had no alternatives. The only thing to do now was to sell his home and spend his life savings on his wife's medical care.

The new unfairness of it all stung him. He had been deprived of a healthy companion for twenty years—that was hard enough. But now he would lose it all for her, everything he owned. There was no end in sight. It was, "Women and children first!"—the cry of all honorable men, and Joey would go down with the *Titanic*.

Sitting in the theater, Joey cried out to God with grief and anger, *God, why are You letting this happen? You could cause things to be different, but they're not.*

Do you hear how Joey's prayer echoes the cry of Jacob?

God had hemmed Joey in. God had the power to change Joey's situation, but for whatever reason, God chose to allow the struggle to continue.

You see, we men love to fix problems. If anything is out of whack, our first response is to roll up our sleeves and tackle the problem. But what happens when we've thrown all we can at it, and the problem is still there? What if trying to fix whatever caused the discouragement isn't the answer?

It's at these times when God says to us most strongly, *I've allowed this discouragement for a reason.* It's in these seasons where God allows all the other springs in our life to dry up. The other springs are areas where we usually go in attempts to feel better. These can be good or bad things—jobs, money, friends, savings, status, power, influence, connections, confidence, dreams, expectations. When these other springs are dried up, the only Spring we have left is God.

This is what Joey was feeling in the theater. He had nothing left. His wife had been taken from him, and all his money and possessions would soon be gone too.

What do we do when we have no other springs left to go to?

Joey remembers praying the heart cry of Moses: "I alone am not able to carry all [this] by myself, it is too burdensome for me" (Num. 11:14). But his prayer seemed unanswered. The only sounds were the credits rolling at the end of the movie and all the people filing out.

Joey tried to get perspective. He felt ashamed to even think such things. It wasn't like he was actually about to die. His circumstances were burdensome, but not lethal.

He went through all he knew to be true: Losing his life savings was not losing his life. He was still alive to give of himself and his resources. And he truly loved his wife. Even though she had been so sick for many years, they still shared a great relationship. Their love was intact, and caring for the wife he loved still felt like a privilege, not a sacrifice.

Life was hard, true, but Joey was not helpless. He was not a victim. He had power. He could make a difference. A strange combination of guilt and thanksgiving swept over him. These extremes of emotion—shame and gratitude—squeezed his heart from both sides. His chest tightened.

Unable to contain the sorrow, he continued to sob.

And unable to contain the joy, he also continued to sob.

This was his spiritual experience: life was hard and God was good. Joey was a strong believer in God. He worked for a Christian publishing company. He knew the Lord was there. Both Sharon and he had an active faith.

Then, in the midst of his sobbing came the perspective that the Lord had sought all along—worship. "Oh, God I praise You," Joey prayed. "Do not let me sink; deliver me . . . from the deep waters" (Ps. 69:14).

This is our invitation too.

It's at the point when all our springs are dried up that God becomes a Fountain. Nothing else can satisfy us. If we're continually driven to try to fix things, God will perpetually allow us to be frustrated until we find rest in Him. But we become energized and renewed by nothing else than relationship with Him.

"Resting" can be a difficult concept for men to grasp. And

it's not a slot-machine-type exchange either—*worship God and all our problems are over.*

We want to be doing, fixing, attacking the problem. But God says the problem will forever be there until we see that He is our only spring of life. God invites us to turn to him and rest in Him, even in the midst of our long-term struggles.

Sometimes this rest can look like silence or quietness, but I rather like to think of resting in the Lord as actively following Him. Resting may not always mean that we sit around and do nothing. Christ doesn't call us to passivity. He calls us through the narrow gate of faith. In Him, we begin to find our strength renewed.

Notice what Joey *didn't* do.

He didn't try to find another doctor to take his wife to. He didn't call his insurance company to put the pressure on. He didn't connive or whine or cheat his way into a temporary "fix." He didn't look to an outside event or activity to mask his pain.

He turned to the Lord in worship.

That's rest.

Resting in the Lord is always a good thing. Christ is an all-capable leader. He knows what He's doing. If we're following Christ, it means we're not making the decisions anymore; the buck doesn't stop with us—it stops with Him. Christ knows exactly where we're going, and we can have full confidence in Him. He is the active commander in charge of the troops. When we follow Him, we arrive at the exact destination where we need to be. Psalm 71:3 describes God as "the rock of refuge" to which we can always go.

And what is the destination He calls us to? It may not be that our problem is solved. It may simply be that our strength is renewed for the challenge. When we follow a mountain guide, the peak doesn't disappear, but we are sure of the route. When we surrender our lives to Christ and follow Him, actively resting in His leadership, Christ rejuvenates our souls so we can continue the journey. The journey may not change, but we will change.

As Joey sat there in the theater, worshipping God, he began to float, not sink. The uplifting presence and peace of God he experienced is tough to put in words. Joey describes it now as the type of incomprehensible sensation that can only come from claiming the promise of Philippians 4:6–7: "Be anxious for nothing, but in everything by prayer and supplication with thanksgiving let your requests be made known to God. And the peace of God, which surpasses all comprehension, shall guard your hearts and your minds in Christ Jesus" (NASB).

Later that day, as he entered the hospital room where his ailing wife rested, she asked, "What has happened to you?" In the glance of an eye, she could read something new on her husband's face.

"I was thinking about how much I love you and thank God for you," Joey told her—and he meant it sincerely. "I am so happy I have you."

Nothing had changed, yet everything had changed. For Joey, giving up his life savings to serve his wife was no longer an issue. That was a done deal. If men on the *Titanic* could sacrifice their lives, then he could sacrifice his life savings. If that was where God was calling him, God was good, and God would provide.

I'm convinced there is a type of intimacy with the Lord we can only know when we struggle with something for a long time. This is the type of peace in the midst of perseverance that the apostle Paul described in 2 Corinthians 12:9–10: "I will boast . . . about my weaknesses, so that Christ's power may rest on me. That is why, for Christ's sake, I delight in weaknesses, in insults, in hardships, in persecutions, in difficulties. For when I am weak, then I am strong."

Joey's story does not end there. As the Lord so often does, He provided Joey with new information. Joey learned that the state would underwrite his medical costs.

Four years have passed, and Joey is a different man. His wife's health has improved too. From time to time his wife still struggles with her illness, but she's doing much better. Joey rejoices over the experience of his long-term suffering. He would not wish it on anyone, yet he would not trade the past with anyone. From it came an experience with the Lord that could have come from nowhere else.

THE STRATEGY OF LAMENT

Resting in the Lord—exchanging our striving for His leadership—is the ultimate call to us when we're in the midst of a long-term season of discouragement. But sometimes it can be difficult to take the leap from despair to worship.

I want to suggest an additional strategy that points us in this direction and keeps us from stepping over the railing. Consider a few thoughts on what active resting in the Lord might look like in your life. Again, resting is not passivity. It is active faith in a good God who has our best interests at heart.

When situations are hard, we may be tempted to call things something other than they are. Well-meaning friends will often encourage us in the midst of hardship to put on a smile, to "buck up" or "just get over it."

I don't believe that's the way to go. God always calls us to name things what they are. He's the God of all truth, and He never asks us to call something what it isn't. If something is sinful, God wants us to call it sinful. If something is absurd or illogical, God doesn't want us to call that thing healthy or whole. Our honesty is always valued by the Lord of all honesty.

So the honest cry in the midst of long-term discouragement becomes, "God, I'm tired of my circumstances." This is the beginning of worship, the cry of lament. It's declaring to the Lord what He already knows is true, that things are not the way they should be. Healthy lament means taking our suffering to the Lord and being honest in His presence. It means trusting Him with our pain, pouring out our distress to Him, and letting Him gradually lead us into a more direct attitude of worship.

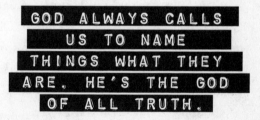

GOD ALWAYS CALLS US TO NAME THINGS WHAT THEY ARE. HE'S THE GOD OF ALL TRUTH.

Lament is something quite different from griping, complaining, and whining. The difference is trust. During the Exodus, the Israelites grew restless when their confidence in Yahweh's goodness and ability waned. Their complaints were really accusations, expressions of mistrust. And those complaints were made *about* the Lord, not *to* the Lord.

True lament is what we see in a lot of the psalms—a gradual shift from complaint to praise and thanksgiving. And that's what I almost always experience when I dare let down my guard, stop ignoring my pain or spouting off to others, and bring my distress directly to God. No matter how painful my distress, my heart eventually turns a corner and moves toward hope. I take my pain to the One who can handle it.

The Lord is big enough to handle our laments. For example, King David admits this type of honesty before the Lord in the midst of long-term discouragement. For years he wanted to be king. God had promised it. But King Saul tried that whole time to kill David instead.

In Psalm 56:8, David prays, "Record my lament; list my tears on your scroll." This is the prayer of a deeply frustrated man. Sometimes we shy away from praying honest prayers like this. But God allows our honesty; He even welcomes it. We don't have to hold back the truth in our hearts from the One who loves us most. This is a good place to start when we're discouraged: we simply lament.

Lamenting is simply being honest before the Lord. And it can take a lot of forms. If you're like me, you might find you have nothing to say when you're frustrated, no words to articulate the depth of the dimensions of your hunger, thirst, disappointment, guilt, or anger.

It's not that we need to pour ashes on our heads or even that we need to cry. I know a lot of men who pour out their lament in very constructive ways. A good friend of mine hits the garden when he's upset. He tills the soil, rips out weeds, and plants things of beauty and purpose in their place. In his mind, gardening is a form of admitting his frustration before the Lord. Other guys I know journal, or do woodworking, or go for a run. They're not looking for solutions to their problems, or even to feel

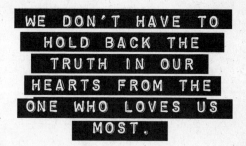

WE DON'T HAVE TO HOLD BACK THE TRUTH IN OUR HEARTS FROM THE ONE WHO LOVES US MOST.

better. They're just pouring out their anger or frustration to a God who cares. They're calling things what they are. Lamenting is the way they grieve the loss over the way things should be.

I love Michael Card's book, *A Sacred Sorrow*, which encourages us to learn "the lost language of lament" and pour out our pain before God. Card writes that complaining can be a form of worship, a way of drawing close to God.[1] It's what Job did. So did the prophet Jeremiah and even Jesus on the cross. The Bible never tells us to just suck it up and bear our pain stoically. Instead, we are told to cast our burdens on the Lord, including our doubt and pain. Until we trust Him with our honest pain and true doubt, we can't receive the gift of His comfort.

I also suggest that in the midst of long-term suffering, we don't try to travel alone. One of the most crucial things we can do if we find ourselves in an extended period of brokenness is to surround ourselves with people who can speak hope to us.

It's at these times that trusted friends can jog our memories when we forget what God has done for us. Or help us see the big picture of what God is doing in our life. In times of extended waiting, the companionship and support of other people can be the Lord's most important provision.

And yes, I know trusted friends are not always easy to come by. Old friendships won't necessarily stand up to new pressures. Church friends, sadly, may be sources of condemnation instead of encouragement. It's hard to reach out to new friends when we're in a place of need. And sometimes it's just hard to meet people, especially if our circumstances have changed.

In a time of long-term discouragement, you might need to ask God to send you the friend you need. I believe He will honor that prayer—although you might need to keep your eyes and heart open, because the person the Lord sends you may not be the kind of person you had in mind.

WRESTLING THE FOUNTAIN

I think it took Jacob awhile to "get it."

After twenty long years looking after sheep for Laban, the Lord released Jacob from that role and told him to go back to the land of his fathers.

Things weren't automatically easy. Laban pursued Jacob and they had some strong words, but eventually the two men came to an understanding. Then Jacob had to go back home and have a fearful meeting with his twin brother Esau, whom he hadn't seen since he had cheated him out of their father's blessing.

But I like to think that while Jacob was still out with the sheep, he was quite close to the truth.

Just before he met Esau, Jacob had one night where he encountered God face to face. It didn't look anything like a worship service. On the face, it was a wrestling match. Around and around, in the blood and the sweat and the grunting and the pushing, Jacob and God wrestled until daybreak.

Jacob couldn't win, and when he knew it, he asked the Wrestler for a blessing.

That was Jacob's turning point.

He had to be stripped of all his springs first, and in his case, that meant his tendency to fight.

When he had nothing left, Jacob turned to the Fountain.

The Fountain didn't destroy him.

In fact, the Fountain blessed him. He changed Jacob's name from "the deceiver," to "he who wrestles with God." The name was a blessing, not a curse. I like to think of it as a gentle reminder of who Jacob used to be and a strong encouragement toward the kind of man the Lord was transforming him into.

That's grace.

The bottom-line message in long-term discouragement is that God sees us and knows the details of our lives. He knows the sins we've committed and the sins done against us. He knows what it's like to be mistreated and rejected, forgotten and despairing. He sees our weariness and desperation in the meantime.

It's in those seasons where the Lord invites us to come to Him. Come to Him with lament. Come to Him with honesty. Accept His leadership, and worship Him as the God of all glory, the One who cares for us always.

REFLECTIONS FOR THOSE WHO CARE
9

TAMMY MALTBY

When someone you know is in the throes of long-term discouragement, you may be tempted to simply tell that person to "buck up." But easy solutions are not what this person needs.

It's important to encourage a person to get checked out physically by a medical doctor. Feelings of hopelessness and isolation that don't go away could be a sign of a chemical imbalance or other physical ailment.

If a physical examination reveals no underlying medical causes, one of the best ways to help a person is to walk through this season with him. It won't be the most fun for either of you. But the Lord's invitation to you may simply be to weather this season of desolation with your friend.

Our hope is always found in the Lord, but it may be difficult for your friend to see this in his darkest days. Encourage your friend to come to the Lord with the honesty of his life. It's okay to tell the Lord that days are difficult. Some of the best times of worship can occur when we worship Him as the God of all glory, the One who cares for us always, even though our lives are miserable right now.

KEY SCRIPTURE

How long, O LORD? Will you forget me forever?
How long will you hide your face from me?
How long must I wrestle with my thoughts
and every day have sorrow in my heart? (Ps. 13:1–2)

WORD OF GRACE

In the sight of God, despair and lament are sometimes the truest forms of trust and worship.

CHAPTER 10

AGENTS OF GRACE
God's Job Description for an Abundant Life

So there you are—you and your friend are sitting across from each other in a coffee shop, or side by side at a baseball game, or leaning across the fence while tinkering with lawn mowers—and you say to your buddy, "So how's it going anyway?"

Maybe his eyes dart to the side, or he takes another swig of beer, or he coughs sort of nervously and says, "Well, actually I've had a tough time lately with . . . "

And suddenly you're into it. You're past the veneer of small talk and into the deeper places of real life.

What happens next?

Men want a job to do—even when talking with a friend. We want to know what to do and when to do it. When it comes to dealing with the hard stuff of life, we don't like to just sit around and do *nothing*. We never like to do that, except maybe when the sitting around involves a couch and a football game on TV. But at least we're still doing something then—we're *actively relaxing*, if you know what I mean.

So what do you do if a buddy comes to you and confesses

that he's dealing with one of the problems discussed in this book, such as lust, infidelity, materialism, substance abuse, or any problem for that matter? What do you do—or not do—to help him along his journey?

Our job frames up like this: God wants us to minister to men who are just like us—who are called to live abundant lives but who are also fully capable of becoming stuck in deadwood. We are given the incredible job of being the Lord's hands and feet and voice and pocketbook on earth. Our job is to live out the ministry of Christ—who Christ is, what He's done, what He's like, and what He continues to do. Our job is to be agents of grace.

It's not always easy. God's call is continually to move us from being good Christian guys in the wrong sense of the phrase—guys who know all the right answers and only run with the right crowd and always try to be nice and safe—to something far more real. We're called to the unsafe place of no more zipped-up religion. No more pretentious happy talk. No more minimizing tricky issues or covering up problems we don't have easy answers for. No more pretending to have it all together for the sake of "witness." We're called into the true depths of real life—and yes, often it's messy. But it's exactly the place where Christ goes. Real life is the place where His light can shine the brightest.

> WE ARE GIVEN THE INCREDIBLE JOB OF BEING THE LORD'S HANDS AND FEET AND VOICE AND POCKETBOOK ON EARTH.

So what does this mean in a practical sense? When it comes to being God's agent of grace, what does our job description look like?

IN TOUGH MOMENTS

A friend of mine, Pete, just experienced this with his seventeen-year-old son, Ryan.

One evening not too long ago, Ryan asked his dad if they could talk privately in the den after dinner. When they sat down together, Pete saw that Ryan had a jittery look in his eyes. Dad knew something was up.

"Ryan, what's going on?" Pete began.

"I don't quite know how to tell you this, Dad," Ryan said, then his eyes got wet and he choked up. Pete told me later he wished he had done the right thing just then, but his mind immediately suspected the worst, and his anger and fear got the best of him.

"Does this have anything to do with Mandy?" Pete asked. "Are you guys in trouble?" Ryan had been dating Mandy, a high school junior, for nearly a year and a half. Pete knew they were getting too close, and they had talked about it on more than one occasion.

Ryan just nodded.

"Is Mandy . . . is she pregnant?"

Ryan nodded again.

Pete snapped. "Haven't you listened to anything I've told you?"

When people confess real-life issues to us, particularly grown children, how tempting it is to want to teach that person a lesson. But Pete says now his first response was one of the worst things he could have done. How you respond to that person, in his or her moment of vulnerability, sticks with that person forever.

With his son crying openly now, Pete paced around his office for several minutes trying to collect his thoughts. He felt in shock, like someone had slammed him with a fist. What would they do now? Both families were Christian. There was no way Ryan and Mandy could get married at their age—it would have compounded their problems, not solved them. Pete felt all the paradoxical astonishment of both extremes of feelings. He was going to be a grandparent for the first time, and a baby is a wonderful blessing, but Pete had never hoped it would happen like this.

That's when Pete decided to do the grace-filled thing—he went back to his son, put his arms around him, and told him they'd get through it together. His son was a Christian. Ryan knew he messed up, but Pete chose to enter Ryan's world, his place of pain. Life would teach any lesson that needed to be taught.

Pete and Ryan were able to simply sit and be silent together for some time. There were no words that would do justice to the moment; they just had to be in each other's changed worlds. After time, they were able to pray together—right there in the den, they got on their knees and sought the Lord's guidance. Then over the next two hours they were able to map out a few next steps of what they might do: talk to Mandy's family, help with medical bills, discuss possibilities for adoption, find out what Mandy's wishes were.

Pete says that those crisis hours with his son turned into a precious time. How he received his son was vital for how his son would forever see how God received him. Pete was able to reaffirm the characteristics of God to Ryan—that God is a God of love, forgiveness, sovereignty, and acceptance.

The situation is far from resolved today, but God continues to redeem the circumstances for His glory. Pete describes it as "the beginning of Ryan's road, the beginning of his story. Ryan wants to be a godly man, and this experience will shape his life forever."

CALLED TO BE REAL

I like that story so much. How Pete chose to respond to his son in the end is exactly what this book is all about. I'm the first one to admit I don't have all the answers for knowing what it means to be an agent of grace, but I believe the Bible gives us several glimpses into this job description.

In the first place, being an agent of grace means we're called to *authenticity*. *Authentic* means genuine. It means real. It means not hiding ourselves behind a facade—even a good Christian facade—but being honest with ourselves and others about our struggles, failures, and weaknesses. And not just the interesting ones. Not just the ones we're pretty sure will be excused or

> BEING AN AGENT OF GRACE MEANS WE'RE CALLED TO AUTHENTICITY.

accepted. But also the messy, embarrassing ones. The ones that make us cringe and squirm just to admit they apply to us.

When Pete talked with Ryan, he was able to talk about some of the times he had messed up as a young man. Those mistakes didn't mean the end of the world for Pete; it just meant he learned from them along the way. The mistakes shaped him—God was able to use them as windows and opportunities for grace. Pete wasn't a perfect father either, and he never claimed to be. But because he realized his own imperfections and spoke about them freely, he was able to see himself and his son on the road of grace together.

Authenticity, in fact, is the whole point of confession. It's a matter of opening our lives to God so we'll find healing . . . and opening our lives to others so we can learn from each other, help each other, speak truth to each other, and share God's healing grace.

The book of 1 John has another name for authenticity. John calls it "living in the light":

> If we are living in the light, as God is in the light, then we have fellowship with each other, and the blood of Jesus, his Son, cleanses us from all sin.
>
> If we claim we have no sin, we are only fooling ourselves and not living in the truth. But if we confess our sins to him, he is faithful and just to forgive us our sins and to cleanse us from all wickedness. (1:7–9 NLT)

Living in the light isn't the same as emotional exhibitionism. It doesn't mean we dump all our issues on any poor soul who happens to be nearby. That kind of over-the-top confession can easily teeter over into reverse pride: *Look how much I've sinned; my life is really awful!* With just a little bit of spin, a confession can become every bit as false as pious hypocrisy, a cover-up for real issues. It can also be abusive, a way of manipulating others: *I'm messed up, so I need you to do things for me.*

A confession is different when a good Christian guy dares to live transparently. This means not hiding in shame or vying for attention, not using one sin to distract from another less embarrassing one, not trying to one-up anyone else's confession.

An authentic confession simply conveys trust in God. It allows His light into the dark places of heart and soul and spirit. It seeks true healing and forgiveness instead of cover-ups and secrecy. And it dares to let other people in on the process.

This kind of authenticity can be hard. Sometimes it feels like humilation rather than humility. We feel exposed and vulnerable. Shallow, surface Christianity starts to look good. Hypocrisy starts to sound like a plan.

But it is only when we dare unveil our deepest pain and shame to ourselves, to Christ, and to others that we break

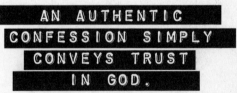

AN AUTHENTIC CONFESSION SIMPLY CONVEYS TRUST IN GOD.

the secrets that bind us, receive grace from the Lord, and find a way to connect to the deep pain of others. Only in this way do we earn the right to be heard and to be trusted.

Not that we'll ever do it perfectly. Not that we'll ever get the balance right. Not that we'll ever break entirely free of sin and self-deceit as long as we're on the earth.

But making the choice to seek the light with our lives makes such a difference. When we strive for authenticity, doing our best to let God's light into the dark places of our souls, we open up our lives—and the lives of others—to the healing flow of God's grace.

CALLED TO COMPASSION

In addition to being authentic, I absolutely believe we're called to be compassionate. Compassion means something different than sympathy or empathy.

Sympathy takes on someone else's burden as one's own. And that is never our call. Even though we (or our wives) often send "sympathy" cards to someone when that person has been hurt, the deeper connotations of sympathy are different from simply identifying with another person's experiences of sorrow. At worst, sympathy is trying to be someone else's savior. We take on the responsibility of fixing that person, or carry his burdens for him, and we will always fail at this.

Our first call is actually to empathy. This is where we see another's sorrow and

> WHEN WE STRIVE FOR AUTHENTICITY, DOING OUR BEST TO LET GOD'S LIGHT INTO THE DARK PLACES OF OUR SOULS, WE—OPEN UP OUR LIVES—AND THE LIVES OF OTHERS—TO THE HEALING FLOW OF GOD'S GRACE.

identify with it. We say (and mean) things like, "Yeah, I can see how that is very hard for you." We still let the other person deal with his situation, but we grasp his sorrow, we understand how he could feel that way, we acknowledge his pain as real and important.

Compassion is when we take our empathy and do something about it. We feel something *and* we act upon it. Being compassionate doesn't mean that we try to fix the other person, or take responsibility for his mistakes. But it means we enter into his world of hurt and try to help. When we extend compassion we try to understand the other person. We see his potential and his pain. We truly listen to his hurt, disappoint-

> COMPASSION IS WHEN WE TAKE OUR EMPATHY AND DO SOMETHING ABOUT IT.

ment, and needs. We genuinely care about his life. We ask what we can do (or not do). And we respond kindly and helpfully to him.

Sometimes compassion comes easiest to us when we've been there ourselves. One way God uses our pain is to teach us what forms of ministry are most helpful.

Compassion is a choice, even for those who have known suffering. We must choose to see. We must choose to reach out to the other person and weep when he weeps. We must choose to build a bridge into another person's life instead of putting up a wall.

We may be called to point the person to a professional who can help: a doctor, a therapist, a lawyer. Sometimes the most compassionate thing we can do is to acknowledge that professional intervention is required.

At its core, compassion means we take the time to notice and care—to listen with our hearts as well as our ears, to weep when another brother weeps (Rom. 12:15 NLT). We don't have to worry about having all the answers or knowing what to say. Simply being there can be one of the greatest forms of ministry ever.

Compassion means that God wants us to move from understanding and caring to practical, hands-on support—doing whatever we can to ease another person's burdens. Compassion applies energy, imagination, and elbow grease to help meet a need.

Jesus's words on this subject are pointed and clear. He stated that when we feed the hungry and clothe the naked and visit prisoners and take care of the sick, we are actually ministering to Him (Matt. 25:31–46). And surely that passage also applies to those who are hungry for a job, naked of confidence, imprisoned by addiction or debt, or sick with stress. Whatever the need, a little thought and prayer will often yield something practical we can do to help.

It could be an invitation to coffee, or mowing someone's lawn when a friend is away. It could be as simple as writing a check to help with someone's mortgage when he's out of work or as complicated as asking a single father and his kids to live with you for a season so they can get on their feet.

Maybe it involves researching respite care facilities, doing someone's taxes, signing up for an Internet program that provides accountability—the possibilities are endless. And I consider prayer to be an intensely practical and effective offering. When you say you'll pray for someone—actually do it. That's a lesson I remind myself of regularly.

The point is, practical care isn't limited to committees at the church, and it's certainly not just for certain categories of people. Anytime you notice a need and take steps to help meet that need—and you do it out of love—you're fulfilling God's call to compassion.

CALLED TO BE RADICAL ENCOURAGERS

Men are often known for their trash talk. Get a bunch of guys out on the basketball court and just watch the insults fly. But even trash talk can have its share of good-naturedness. As agents of grace, our job description calls us to be encouragers.

To encourage someone means to help a person have courage or confidence or strength. When we encourage others we prompt them to keep doing what's right and to draw closer to God, no matter their circumstances.

I think of encouragement as a ministry of motivation. It's what happens when you notice someone's steps are faltering and then come alongside to help him keep moving forward. Encouragement is about standing side by side with another person to give him strength in battle.

ANYTIME YOU NOTICE A NEED AND TAKE STEPS TO HELP MEET THAT NEED—AND YOU DO IT OUT OF LOVE—YOU'RE FULFILLING GOD'S CALL TO COMPASSION.

And the best thing about this kind of encouragement is that it's a two-way street. One day I'm the encourager, the next day I'm the one in need of a boost. So we move forward together, ministering grace to one another. In the words of Hebrews 10:24, we "spur one another on toward love and good deeds."

There are so many ways to be an encourager—a word of confidence, a slap on the back that reminds a guy he's not alone, a well-placed note or well-timed e-mail that says you're praying for him, even an honest comment that helps shift his perspective and focus his goals. Sometimes it's just a simple reminder that things will get better.

But sometimes encouragement needs to get radical.

Before a friend of mine got married, he roomed with several guys in a big house downtown in order to save expenses. The guys were all in their late twenties and had their own lives and jobs by then. They were all Christians and devoted to the Lord.

But when one of the guy's girlfriends left him, things began to sour. The guy (not my friend, but one of the guys in the house) had grown up in the state foster care system and struggled with expressing true grief. He really cared for his girlfriend, but she had chosen to take another path.

> SOMETIMES ENCOURAGEMENT NEEDS TO GET RADICAL.

The friends tried to cheer up their roommate. Sometimes he was snappy or depressed. They let him have his space. Sometimes he needed to talk. They stayed up nights listening to him.

Their encouragement was stretched even further when a policeman showed up one day at their front door. The roommate was questioned, then let go with a promise to appear in court on a certain time and day. When the policeman left, the roommate came clean with the other guys in the house.

It seems he had a secret addiction to porn that had taken some drastic turns. Whenever the roommate felt depressed or angry, he turned to sexuality in an attempt to feel better. It had been a lifelong pattern that had only worsened over time. When the girlfriend had dumped him, it had really sent him over the edge. One day while out in his car, he had exposed himself to some teenage girls. The teens had written down his license plate number and called the police.

When my friend heard this, he was truly saddened—and he, along with all the other guys in the house, had a choice to make. They could kick the guy out of the house, or they could all choose to support their friend through this tough time, even though he had chosen some really wrong paths.

Encouragement can be like that. The call to encouragement can take us far from our comfort 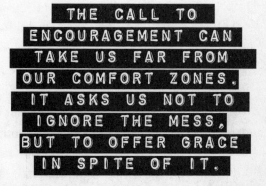 zones. It asks us not to ignore the mess, but to offer grace in spite of it. Encouragement reflects the nature of God. He is always willing that we turn to him, no matter what we've done.

My friend and his housemates chose to love and support their friend. They didn't kick him out, but they tried as much as they could to walk through that difficult season with him. Over the next several months they listened to him, prayed with him, helped him set boundaries, and loaned him money when his legal bills became more than he could handle. Most of all, they reminded him that he wasn't a pervert (which is what he said he felt like a lot of the time); the Lord still loved him and could use his life for good.

Today that housemate is happily married and in a stable career. His life isn't perfect, but my friend likes to think that a little radical encouragement in a season of need went a long way, and was part of the healing that helped this guy make it through.

CALLED TO RECONCILIATION

Part of our job description is the call to what the apostle Paul called a "ministry of reconciliation" (2 Cor. 5:18).

Reconcile is a word used for settling arguments, bringing harmony out of discord, restoring strained relationships, and bringing peace. Its root meaning is to repair or to make good again, and it usually refers to healing or restoring relationships.

As agents of grace, we're called to be ministers of reconciliation—that means we help bring new life to people by helping restore their relationships with God and each other. Or more accurately, we relate to people in such a way that they're more open to God's reconciling and renewing work in their lives.

Paul explains it this way:

> Therefore, if anyone is in Christ, he is a new creation; the old has gone, the new has come! All this is from God, who reconciled us to himself through Christ and gave us the ministry of reconciliation: that God was reconciling the world to himself in Christ, not counting men's sins against them. And he has committed to us the message of reconciliation. We are therefore Christ's ambassadors, as though God were making his appeal through us. (2 Cor. 5:17–20)

God's the one who does the real restorative work in people's lives. But we're the messengers, the ambassadors, the go-betweens. Our job is to build relationships, make connections, and establish a presence in people's lives so that God can restore their relationship with Him and with others. This ministry isn't just to unbelievers. I believe we're also called to reach out to our fellow Christians who have lost their way and become estranged from God.

How do we carry out this healing work? Partly through our words—our authentic attempts to explain the changes that have come into our lives because of Christ. And also by the way we live—through our honesty, compassion, practical help, and encouragement.

First Peter 3:15–16 describes an effective ministry of reconciliation: "Worship Christ as Lord of your life. And if someone asks about your Christian hope, always be ready to explain it. But do this in a gentle and respectful way" (NLT).

Of course, one of the most powerful ways to reconcile others with God is to make reconciliation a priority in our own lives—that means being willing to extend mercy and forgiveness to those who have hurt us, seeking forgiveness from those we have hurt and from God, seeking to reconcile our own painful and broken relationships.

We won't always succeed right away, because true forgiveness often takes time and healing. We may not succeed at all in certain cases, because reconciliation requires the willingness of both parties. But the more we make the ministry of reconciliation a priority in our lives, the stronger our relationship with the Lord will grow.

CALLED TO COURAGE

It's always easier to observe pain from a distance than it is to roll up our sleeves and step forward to help. But I believe as men of God, we need to be proactive in our commitment to help others when they're in need.

It's definitely harder to step into another person's life to confront him, to care for him, to be available and love him to the truth, but this is our call, our invitation, and our privilege.

True ministry is seldom easy. Love for others brought a scourge to Christ's back and a cross to His ministry. Barbara Brown Taylor says if our love isn't a suffering love, a love that suffers and grieves and hurts, then we're doing something wrong.[1] As we follow Christ, He will ask us to go into some hurtful places with others. Christ never says His way will be easy, but He does say it will be fulfilling, purposeful, and abundant.

I've experienced this call lately with a good friend of mine. I'll call him Duke.

Duke is a prominent Christian who has developed a drinking problem over the years that has finally come to a head. Word has gotten around town lately that Duke has been involved in some activities he shouldn't, including sleeping around on his wife. There have been a lot of behind-the-back accusations, gossip, and rumors, even by some people who considered Duke their friend. But I haven't seen much evidence of anybody stepping up to the plate and relating to Duke with the principles of Matthew 18:15–16:

> If your brother sins against you, go and show him his fault, just between the two of you. If he listens to you, you have won your brother over. But if he will not listen, take one or two others along, so that every matter may be established by the testimony of two or three witnesses.

As I have continued to hear talk of Duke's escapades, I kept sensing that I needed to step up to the plate and go talk to Duke, face to face. At one time he had professed to follow Christ closely—had he forgotten all that? I had no idea what I would say to him. I didn't know if he would listen to me or try to take a swing at me. I just knew I needed to go talk to him to see if I could help.

The day I drove over to his house, I have to admit I was scared. And this is always the way it is anytime we speak to a brother in love—it's inconvenient, there's a cost to us, we always run the risk of being misunderstood, yelled at, or worse. When I rang the doorbell, I had no idea what I'd find.

Minutes went by with my heart ticking. Finally Duke appeared. He looked like he had been out drinking all night. His hair was sticking up all over, he was bleary eyed, and he seemed hungover.

Duke is a big man, heavyset and muscular, well over six feet tall—definitely one not known for expressing his emotions, but when he saw it was me at the front door, he immediately embraced me, thanked me for coming over, and began to weep. I have no great remembrance of what we said to each other that afternoon. But I believe that Duke responded to a small degree to the love and concern that was shown him that day.

I wish I could write today that Duke is doing better. In many ways, he's still wandering far from his Father God. My consolation is to know that God is always there for Duke. The Lord hasn't forgotten about him, and the door of grace is always open.

As for us, this is a reminder of the call of Christ. It's not my job to "fix" Duke, but it is my job to care for him as my brother, no matter what sort of mess he's into. I know it's hard to step into another person's life, but this type of proactive courage is our invitation as agents of grace.

Sometimes it can be overwhelming. Need is always all around us. And perhaps the general principle here is to begin small—with one friend, one brother in need. We are not all called to minister to the masses, but we are all invited to step forward to help one guy in our lives who needs a helping hand.

What God Can Do with Your Yes

This is the message of this book: as good Christian guys, we're all called to live real and authentic lives. That's what a true confession is about.

When we confess we develop a lifestyle of authenticity. We don't use grace as a license to sin, but we know that when we do stray, there is a loving God who always invites us home.

And this grace gives us the guts to extend compassion to those who are hurting, to offer help when needed, to radically encourage those who need a word of grace. We're all called to be Christ's ambassa-

> THIS IS THE MESSAGE OF THIS BOOK: AS GOOD CHRISTIAN GUYS, WE'RE ALL CALLED TO LIVE REAL AND AUTHENTIC LIVES. THAT'S WHAT A TRUE CONFESSION IS ABOUT.

dors, living in such a way that we help restore people's relationships to God and each other.

It goes without saying we won't always get it right. This book is not about trying to shine ourselves up as Christians. In fact, if you're anything like me, you're bound to get it wrong a lot of the time.

I hope we realize that's okay.

I don't say that to minimize sin; I say it as the reality of our lives. Hebrews 12:1 encourages us to "throw off . . . the sin that so easily entangles." The directive is to stop sinning, but the acknowledgment is that sin is sticky business indeed.

And that's life. You won't always have the courage to live authentically. Sometimes you'll be so caught up in denial that you won't even know you're being dishonest. Or you'll be so paralyzed by fear that you just can't face admitting your failures to another person. You'll fail to speak the truth as you understand it—or you'll speak the truth harshly and alienate people instead of drawing them to God.

Sometimes you won't always have the insight or the energy—or even the interest—to be compassionate. Or your pain will loom so large you'll have a hard time caring about somebody else's suffering. Or you'll hide from your own sins by obsessing over others' failures, offering them judgment and condemnation instead of grace and compassion.

Sometimes you'll be too busy or preoccupied or just plain selfish to reach out in practical ways, too mired in your own sense of inadequacy to encourage someone else, too angry at God or someone else to even consider being a reconciler. Sometimes you won't even want to try.

And yes, sometimes I'll be there too. Multiple times. It's the true world that good Christian guys live in.

The good news is that we don't have to look good on the outside in order for God to use us. All we have to be is willing. All we really have to say is yes . . . and He'll take us from there.

God can do so much with a yes! He doesn't ever require us to be perfect—perfecting us is His job. But because He's given us free will, He won't do a thing with us until we say yes to Him.

Yes to what He wants to do in our lives.

Yes to letting Him change us and shape our destiny.

Yes to learning and adopting His point of view and sharing His concerns.

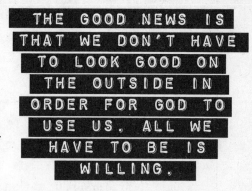

THE GOOD NEWS IS THAT WE DON'T HAVE TO LOOK GOOD ON THE OUTSIDE IN ORDER FOR GOD TO USE US. ALL WE HAVE TO BE IS WILLING.

Yes to trying to be authentic and compassionate and practically helpful and encouraging and reconciling.

Yes to letting Him heal and comfort us "in all our troubles so that we can comfort others" (2 Cor. 1:4 NLT).

Yes to letting Him forgive our failures to get it right!

And yes to His view of what our part is in all of it—because that's one of the hardest things for any of us to get right. We just can't seem to keep straight what we're called to do and what God wants to do. That's why His call seems too overwhelming at times. That's why we get so weary in well-doing, why we burn out. That's why we turn into control freaks or fail to live up to our promises—or both! We keep trying to do God's job instead of ours.

You see, it's not our place to fix people or to save their souls. It's not our place to convict them of sin or grant them forgiveness (though we may be called to speak truthfully about sin and grace).

All that is God's job—and He does it beautifully. He's the one in charge of the whole process. He's the one who works through us to love and guide others. And of course He's the one who keeps caring for us in all our roller-coaster ups and downs.

So what is our job description? It's really a lot simpler than we think it is.

Our job is to listen to Him.

Our job is to obey Him.

Our job is to step out in faith, moving forward even when we don't think we can.

Our job is to keep coming to Him for help and comfort and forgiveness.

And our job, most of all, is to remember who we are . . . and who God is.

And then to get ourselves out of the way so God can do His work.

REFLECTIONS FOR THOSE
WHO CARE
10

T A M M Y   M A L T B Y

When someone talks to us about the deep issues of his life, it's easy to want to give advice or resort to a "better than thou" mind-set. But the key is to see another's mistakes with the same eyes that we see our own. We've all overstepped the mark; we've all been disobedient and fallen short of the glory of God. The grace we've once received is a reminder to freely give grace away. We walk this road together.

The call to be agents of grace is really an invitation to humility—it is a tremendous privilege, yet it is also a tremendous reminder that we are all saved by Christ's amazing grace.

Our call is to be aware of Christ's unending love, thankful that grace extends to us always, and worshipful of a great God who runs down the road in search of us, His arms open wide.

KEY SCRIPTURE

Confess your sins to each other and pray for each other so that you may be healed. (James 6:16)

WORD OF GRACE

Not, "There but for the grace of God go I."
But, "There in the grace of God . . . we go together."

Notes from the Back of a Truck

If I could make sure you remember one thing from this book, it would be this—as good Christian guys, *confession will always be a way of life for us.*

We will always have areas of deadwood in our lives. We will always be called to rip away the falsely righteous facades that tempt us and to talk honestly about what's truly happening in our lives. Sin flourishes wherever there are secrets. Hope, strength, and an abundant life are found when grace is received and those secrets are torn away.

Hopefully, our struggles diminish as we grow to be more like Christ—our battles with sin become less frequent as we learn to live victoriously. But I don't think we ever fully arrive at our destination, this side of heaven. That's what grace is always about. We always need it. And it's always available to us. That's the message of this book. Grace is truly amazing. We need it like we need our next breath.

Do we have a responsibility involved in grace? Absolutely. We're not victims, and we're not couch-sitters. Living a grace-filled life still means we take 100 percent responsibility for our actions. It means with Christ's help we can create a strategy to become whole. Christ is the ultimate Healer. Yet He invites us along in our journey toward becoming the men of God we're called to be.

Grace is all about God's extreme love for us. And grace is always the final answer. Grace is God's reaching to us no matter

who we are, where we are, or what we've done. God loves us—
period. He hates our sin, but Christ took the penalty of sin for
us on the cross. When we sin, God is always the good Father to
us, like the Father of the prodigal son, who fervently searches the
horizon for us, longing for us to return.

Living in grace means our lives probably won't look tidy anymore. They don't need to. Desiring the appearance of a tidy life
can be one of the greatest hindrances to the true righteousness
Christ offers. Henri Nouwen, the great writer of a variety of books
on spiritual development, prayer, and contemplation, described
the grace-filled lifestyle as living the life of a "wounded healer."[1]

A wounded healer lives abundantly in spite of brokenness. In
fact, this same untidiness can give a person compassion and
understanding to serve and minister to others in need. Through
serving, through pouring out our lives, our areas of brokenness
can become healed. Christ instructed his disciples to, "Give, and
it will be given to you. A good measure, pressed down, shaken
together and running over, will be poured into your lap. For with
the measure you use, it will be measured to you" (Luke 6:38).

This outward look to serve others can take a lot of forms.
Our call might be to serve the literal neighbor down our street.
Or it may be a more metaphoric neighbor, such as the "neigh-
bor" who lives in the country next to ours.

Scripture teaches that God's heart is aligned with the needs
of the poor, the widow, the stranger, and the orphan. God has an
incredible passion for these people because they are the most
marginalized in our world. They are alone, hungry, hurting, and
in desperate need of other Christ-followers to reveal the love of
Christ to them in touchable, practical, real-life ways. James 1:27

speaks boldly of Christ's heart in this area: "Religion that God our Father accepts as pure and faultless is this: to look after orphans and widows in their distress."

As a fatherless child myself, someone who didn't know his real dad for sixteen years, I carried many father-wounds with me into my adult life. Some of those wounds have been healed as I prayed and trusted God to teach me to be a husband and a father and as I've looked to other men I respect and admire to help fill the gaps of experience and knowledge I didn't possess.

But some of the pain has remained from the loss. A few festering injuries continue to emerge from time to time. I feel the pain of this, and no one's life—including mine—is ever free of struggles.

Further healing continues to take place in my life as I serve others who struggle like me and worse than me. Today I minister out of a place of my weakness rather than my strength. I find great comfort in Jesus's words, recorded in 2 Corinthians 12:9: "My grace is sufficient for you, for my power is made perfect in weakness."

There is a mystery that occurs when we are weak. And there is a special grace when we are strong enough to admit we need help. We need God to help us overcome the struggles we face on a daily basis. When we surrender our weaknesses to God, He shows Himself strong.

WELCOME TO THE JOURNEY

What is my life like today?

God has brought me out of a childhood of neglect and abuse, and a young adulthood of drugs and crime, to live an abundant life.

It doesn't mean I'm perfect.

It means I live in grace.

God is my all. I say that without hesitation. He is better than anything I could ever imagine, and every day I surrender my life to His plan.

And God invites me to serve. And as I serve, my pain is caught by the Great Physician, who transforms it into compassion, understanding, and power to help make a difference.

As I am writing this, I'm very literally bouncing in the back of a truck along a dirt road in Swaziland, Africa, the home of the highest rate of HIV/AIDS in the world, over 44 percent. I'm here for ten days with a team of several others, surveying orphanages and various projects in an attempt to learn more and help wherever we can. Almost half of the population here will be dead in five to seven years, and soon there will be few left except orphaned children. As a Christ-follower, I just can't stand by and watch this happen.

I'm not here out of my strength. This isn't the Tom Davis mission. I'm here because I'm weak and I need God to be strong in my life. I'm here because I truly believe that pure religion is helping widows and orphans in their distress. I know it matters to God, and I believe that by being a wounded healer, my wounds can be healed.

That's my life for today.

How about you?

Whatever abundant calling God has for you, the journey is worth it. The pain you've experienced, and perhaps are still encountering today, can be turned into blessing and redemption. Don't give up. Stay the course, fight the fight of faith, and follow the Lord of all grace on the amazing journey He has for you.

APPENDIX

Resources for Further Help

www.aacc.net The American Association of Christian Counselors Web site. This site offers helpful articles on a number of topics plus help in finding a reputable Christian counselor.

www.suicidepreventionlifeline.org *National Suicide Prevention Lifeline.* This confidential, twenty-four-hour service routes callers to local crisis centers across the country. For more information call the hotline at 1-800-273-TALK (8255).

www.TroubledWith.com. This excellent site, sponsored by Focus on the Family, provides articles, resources, and referrals on a number of family-related topics including abuse and addiction, life pressures, love and sex, parenting, relationships, and transitions.

Resources to Help You Learn More about Grace

Dorrell, Jimmy. *Trolls and Truth: 14 Realities about Today's Church That We Don't Want to See.* Birmingham, AL: New Hope, 2006.

Gire, Ken. *Windows of the Soul.* Grand Rapids: Zondervan, 1996.

Graham, Ruth with Stacy Mattingly. *In Every Pew Sits a Broken Heart: Hope for the Hurting.* Grand Rapids: Zondervan, 2004.

Larkin, Nate. *Samson and the Pirate Monks: Calling Men to Authentic Brotherhood.* Nashville: Thomas Nelson, 2007

Manning, Brennan. *Abba's Child: The Cry of the Heart for Intimate Belonging.* Colorado Springs: NavPress, 2002.

Manning, Brennan. *The Ragamuffin Gospel: Good News for the Bedraggled, Beat-Up, and Burned Out.* Sisters, OR: Multnomah, 2005.

Nouwen, Henri. *The Wounded Healer.* New York: Doubleday, 1979.

Yancey, Philip. *What's So Amazing about Grace?* Grand Rapids: Zondervan, 1997.

Resources for Help with Sexuality Issues

Allender, Dan B. *The Wounded Heart: Hope for Adult Victims of Childhood Sexual Abuse.* Colorado Springs: NavPress, 1990

Anderson, Neil. *Released from Bondage.* Nashville: Thomas Nelson, 2002.

Arterburn, Stephen, Fred Stoeker, and Mike Yorkey. *Every Man's Battle: Winning the War on Sexual Temptation One Victory at a Time.* Colorado Springs: WaterBrook, 2000.

Harris, Joshua. *Not Even A Hint.* Sisters, OR: Multnomah, 2003.

Laaser, Mark R. *Healing Wounds of Sexual Addiction.* Grand Rapids: Zondervan, 2004.

Langberg, Diane. *On the Threshold of Hope: Opening the Door to Healing for Survivors of Sexual Abuse.* Carol Stream, IL: Tyndale, 1999.

MacDonald, Gordon. *When Men Think Private Thoughts.* Nashville: Thomas Nelson, 1997.

Means, Patrick. *Men's Secret Wars.* Grand Rapids: Baker, 2006.

Schaumburg, Harry W. *False Intimacy: Understanding the Struggle of Sexual Addiction.* Colorado Springs: NavPress, 1992.

273

Willingham, Russell. *Breaking Free: Understanding Sexual Addiction and the Healing Power of Jesus.* Downers Grove, IL: InterVarsity, 1999.

www.x3watch.com Offers a free online accountability program.

Resources to Help with Anger, Rage, and Abuse

National Domestic Violence Hotline: 800-799-SAFE (7233).

Branson, Brenda and Paula Silva, "Domestic Violence Among Believers: Confronting the Destructive Secret." *Christian Counseling Today.* Vol. 13 (2005), 3:24–27. Access online at http://www.focusministries1.org/pdf/CCT2005.pdf. The Focus Ministries Web site (http://www.focusministries.org) provides a wealth of excellent help for Christian women.

Chapman, Gary. *The Other Side of Love: Handling Anger in a Godly Way.* Chicago: Moody, 1999.

Miles, Al. *Violence in Families: What Every Christian Needs to Know.* Minneapolis: Augsburg Fortress, 2002.

Safeplace Ministries Web site. An excellent source of information and help on many different kinds of abuse. Access at http://www.safeplace.com (not www.safeplace.org.)

Help for a Father-Wound and Parenting Issues

Chapman, Gary. *The Five Love Languages of Teenagers.* Chicago: Moody, 2000.

Clinton, Tim and Gary Sibcy. *Attachments: Why You Love, Feel, and ACT the Way You Do: Unlock the Secret to Loving and Lasting Relationships.* Brentwood, TN: Integrity, 2002.

Clinton, Tim and Gary Sibcy. *Loving Your Child Too Much: Raise Your Kids without Overindulging, Overprotecting or Overcontrolling.* Nashville: Thomas Nelson, 2006.

Dobson, James. *The New Hide or Seek: Building Self-Esteem in Your Child.* Grand Rapids: Baker, 2001.

Oliver, Gary, and Carrie Oliver. *Raising Sons and Loving It! Helping Your Boys Become Godly Men.* Grand Rapids: Zondervan, 2002.

Rainey, Dennis, and Barbara Rainey. *Parenting Today's Adolescent.* Nashville: Thomas Nelson, 2002.

Trent, John, and Rick Osborne, Kurt Bruner. *A Parents' Guide to the Spiritual Growth of Children.* Carol Stream, IL: Tyndale, 2003.

Veerman, Dave, and Bruce Barton. *When Your Father Dies.* Nashville: Thomas Nelson, 2003.

Evans, Jimmy. *Dealing with Abandonment.* Access at http://www.growthtrac.com/artman/publish/article_568.php

DivorceCare Web site. Excellent site featuring helpful information on groups and dealing with kids. Access at http://divorcecare.com.

Growthtrac Web site. This site (http://www.growthtrac.com) offers some excellent articles on living through failed relationships as well as help for strengthening a struggling relationship. Access the divorce articles at http://www.growthtrac.com/artman/topics/10.php.

Resources for Help with Substance Abuse

12-Step.org Web site. This Web site is a good place to start for information about the many recovery programs based on the "Twelve Step" recovery model of Alcoholics Anonymous. Includes a list of specifically Christian resources. Access online at http://www.12step.org.

Alcoholics Anonymous World Services. *Alcoholics Anonymous.* 4th ed. New York: Alcoholics Anonymous World Services, 2001 (original copyright 1939). Access online at http://www.aa.org/bigbookonline.

Baker, John. *Stepping Out of Denial into God's Grace, Participant's Guide #1*, Celebrate Recovery Program. Grand Rapids: Zondervan, 2004.

Baker, John. *Taking an Honest and Spiritual Inventory, Participant's Guide #1*, Celebrate Recovery
Program. Grand Rapids: Zondervan, 2004.

Baker, John. *Getting Right with God, Yourself, and Others, Participant's Guide #1*, Celebrate
Recovery Program. Grand Rapids: Zondervan, 2004.

Baker, John. *Growing in Christ While Helping Others, Participant's Guide #1*, Celebrate Recovery
Program. Grand Rapids: Zondervan, 2004.

Celebrate Recovery. This Christ-centered "twelve-step" recovery program originated in Lake Forest,
California's Saddleback Church and has been duplicated in more than five hundred churches
across the nation. Celebrate Recovery applies biblical principles and small group support to help
people grow spiritually and break free from addictive, compulsive, and dysfunctional behaviors.
More information on this program can be found in the four books listed above and at
http://www.celebraterecovery.com.

Beattie, Melody. *Codependents' Guide to the 12 Steps: How to Find the Right Program for You and
Apply Each of the Twelve Steps to Your Own Issues.* New York: Simon and Schuster, 1998.

Dodes, Lance M. *The Heart of Addiction: A New Approach to Understanding and Managing
Alcoholism and Other Addictive Behaviors.* New York: HarperCollins, 2002.

Laaser, Mark R. and George Ohlschlager. *Addictions: A Multifaceted Christian Approach.*
Access online at http://aacc.net/2006/08/02/addictions-a-multifaceted-christian-approach/

May, Gerald. *Addiction and Grace.* San Francisco: HarperSanFrancisco, 1988.

Miller, J. Keith. *A Hunger for Healing: The Twelve Steps as a Classic Model for Christian Spiritual
Growth.* San Francisco: HarperSanFrancisco, 1991.

Minirth, Frank et. al. *Love Hunger: Breaking Free from Food Addiction.* Nashville: Nelson Impact,
2004.

Spickard, Anderson and Barbara R. Thompson. *Dying for a Drink: What You and Your Family
Should Know about Alcoholism.* Nashville: W, 2005.

Stoop, David A. and Stephen Arterburn. *Twelve Step Life Recovery Devotional: Thirty Meditations
from Scripture for Each Step in Recovery.* Wheaton, IL: Tyndale, 1991.

Thompson, Tom. "Myth 2: 'Addiction Is Not a Sickness; It Is Simply Repetitive Sin." Article on
American Association of Christian Counselors Web site. Access online at http://aacc.net/2006/
04/11/myth-2-%e2%80%9caddiction-is-not-a-sickness-it-is-simply-repetitive-sin%e2%80%9d/

Resources to Help Sort Out Emotions

Bloem, Steve and Robyn Bloem. *Broken Minds: Hope for Healing When You Feel Like You're "Losing It."*
Grand Rapids: Kregel, 2005.

Cloud, Henry, Dr. and Dr. John Townsend. *Boundaries in Marriage.* Grand Rapids: Zondervan,
2002.

Hegstrom, Paul. *Broken Children, Grown Up Pain: Understanding the Effects of Your Wounded Past.*
Kansas City, MO: Beacon Hill, 2005.

Swenson, Richard. *Margin: Restoring Emotional, Physical, Financial, and Time Reserves to Overloaded
Lives.* Colorado Springs: Navpress, 2004.

Resources to Help with Long-Term Discouragement

Anderson, Fil. *Running on Empty: Contemplative Spirituality for Overachievers.* New York:
WaterBrook, 2004.

Anderson, Neil and Joanne Anderson. *Overcoming Depression.* Ventura, CA: Gospel Light, 2004.

Card, Michael. *A Sacred Sorrow: Reaching Out to God in the Lost Language of Lament.* Colorado
Springs: NavPress, 2005.

Carter, Les. *The Freedom from Depression Workbook.* Nashville: Thomas Nelson, 1996.

Gire, Ken. *The North Face of God: Hope for the Times When God Seems Indifferent.* Wheaton, IL: Tyndale, 2005.

Hart, Archibald. *Unmasking Male Depression.* Nashville: Thomas Nelson, 2001.

Rohr, Richard. *Simplicity: The Freedom of Letting Go,* rev. ed. New York: Crossroad, 2004.

Sorge, Bob. *Secrets of the Secret Place: Keys to Igniting Your Personal Time with God.* Greenwood, MO: Oasis, 2001.

Resources for Help with Pride

Dyson, Michael Eric. *Pride: The Seven Deadly Sins.* New York: Oxford University Press, 2006.

Murray, Andrew. *Humility: The Journey Toward Holiness.* Minneapolis: Bethany, 2001.

Resources for Help with Materialism

Alcorn, Randy. *The Treasure Principle.* Sisters, OR: Multnomah, 2005.

Alcorn, Randy. *Money, Possessions and Eternity.* Sisters, OR: Multnomah, 2003.

Erre, Mike. *The Jesus of Suburbia: Have We Tamed the Son of God to Fit Our Lifestyle?* Nashville: W, 2006.

Hsu, Albert. *The Suburban Christian: Finding Spiritual Vitality in the Land of Plenty.* Downers Grove, IL: InterVarsity, 2006.

NOTES

Passing the Baton

1. Tammy Maltby and Anne Christian Buchanan, *Confessions of a Good Christian Girl: The Secrets Women Keep and the Grace That Saves Them* (Nashville: Thomas Nelson, 2007).

2. Brennan Manning, *The Ragamuffin Gospel: Good News for the Bedraggled, Beat-Up, and Burned Out* (Sisters, OR: Multnomah, 2005), PAGE NUMBER TO COME FROM AUTHORS.

Chapter 2: "I've Got a Dirty Mind"

1. Statistics available at http://www.crosswalk.com/faith/1224639.html, accessed 13 December 2006; http://www.blazinggrace.org/pornstatistics.htm, accessed 13 December 2006.

2. Dolf Zillman and Jennings Jaredt, "Pornography, Sexual Callousness, and the Trivialization of Rape," *Journal of Communications* 32 (1982): 15. Reported in http://www.leaderu.com/orgs/probe/docs/pornplag.html, accessed 13 December 2006.

3. Testimony by John B. Rabun, deputy director, National Center for Missing and Exploited Children, before the Subcommittee on Juvenile Justice of the Senate Judiciary Committee, 12 September 1984. W. Marshall, "Pornography and Sex Offenders," in Dolf Zillman and Jennings Jaredt, eds., *Pornography: Research Advances and Policy Considerations* (New York: Academic Press, 1989). "The Men Who Murdered," *FBI Law Enforcement Bulletin*, August 1985. Reported in http://www.leaderu.com/orgs/probe/docs/pornplag.html, accessed 13 December 2006.

4. Stephen Arterburn, Fred Stoeker, and Mike Yorkey. *Every Man's Battle: Winning the War on Sexual Temptation One Victory at a Time* (Colorado Springs: WaterBrook, 2000), see chapter 11, "Bouncing the Eyes."

5. Ravi Zacharias, *"Pleasure at a Price"* © 2007 Ravi Zacharias International Ministries. http://www.rzim.org/slice/slicetran.php?sliceid=64, accessed 15 March 2007.

6. Elizabeth Crews, *Made for the Master* (Chula Vista, CA: Word Weaver, 2006), 96.

Chapter 3: "I'm a Self-Made Man"

1. These three quotes were taken from http://www.pietyhilldesign.com/gcq/quotepages/pride.html, accessed 01/03/07.

Chapter 4: "I Want More Stuff"

1. Anglican, *The Book of Common Prayer*. Available at http://www.stlukesrec.org/audioprayerbook/Friday_Morning_Prayer.htm, accessed 15 March 2007.

Chapter 5: "I Need My Dad"

1. Fathers Unite, http://www.fathersunite.org/statistics_on_fatherlessnes.html, accessed 15 March 2007.

2. Frederick Buechner, *The Magnificent Defeat* (San Francisco, HarperSanFrancisco, 1985), 65.

Chapter 6: "I Love Booze"

1. Mark R. Laaser and George Ohlschlager, "Addictions: A Multifaceted Christian Approach," http://aacc.net/2006/08/02/addictions-a-multifaceted-christian-approach, accessed 9 February 2007.

Chapter 9: "I Want to Give Up"

1. Michael Card, *A Sacred Sorrow: Reaching Out to God in the Lost Language of Lament* (Colorado Springs: NavPress, 2005).

Chapter 10: Agents of Grace

1. Barbara Brown Taylor, *Leaving Church: A Memoir of Faith* (HarperSanFrancisco, 2007), 215.

A Final Word: Notes from the Back of a Truck

1. Henri Nouwen, *The Wounded Healer: Ministry in Contemporary Society* (New York: Doubleday, 1979).